Like a Shock of Wheat

Like a Shock of Wheat

Meditations on Death

Marvin Hein

Introduction by David Hubbard

90

HERALD PRESS
Scottdale, Pennsylvania
Kitchener, Ontario
1981

Library of Congress Cataloging in Publication Data

Hein, Marvin.
    Like a shock of wheat.

    1. Death—Meditations. I. Title.
BT825.H36   236'.1   80-22224
ISBN 0-8361-1938-X

LIKE A SHOCK OF WHEAT
Copyright © 1981 by Herald Press, Scottdale, Pa. 15683
    Published simultaneously in Canada by Herald Press,
    Kitchener, Ont. N2G 4M5
Library of Congress Catalog Card Number: 80-22224
International Standard Book Number: 0-8361-1938-X
Printed in the United States of America
Design: Alice B. Shetler / Cover Photo: Paul M. Schrock

81 82 83 84 85 10 9 8 7 6 5 4 3 2 1

Dedicated
to the memory of
my Dad, David Hein,
who through 30 years of battling Parkinson's Disease
taught me much about death and life

and to

my wife's father, Dan Martens,
whose death directed my attention to Job 5:26
from which the title of this book comes

Contents

Introduction

Have you truly caught the meaning of the Christian faith? That question is not to be answered lightly. The stakes are momentous, and the evidences of its answer, in my life at least, are ambiguous.

But I can propose several responses. I can, for instance, respond in terms of Christian *information*—Bible verses committed to memory, chronologies and maps learned by rote, creeds and doctrinal definitions recited on demand. My old Sunday school space (not to be dignified by calling it a room) was bounded by a burlap screen to which were tacked ribbons proudly flying the innumerable stickers which marked my feats of learning.

Forty years later, I can express gratitude for the patience and discipline of those teachers who, often without my full cooperation, needled, cajoled, threatened, and bribed me to stow away substantial amounts of information. I have used every squib of it and yearned for more. But I would not cite it as evidence of my understanding of what it means to be a Christian.

A second response is worth trying—a response that calls attention to habits of Christian *piety*. I can seek to test my maturity in things spiritual by noting my inclination to prayer, attendance at church, and commitment to Bible study. From childhood this has been my pattern. Piety was one of the many things I learned at my mother's knee.

In no way would I want to part with this heritage. It has helped to nurture me through the decades in the knowledge and love of God. But pious habits alone may be more a mark of compulsiveness than of maturity; they may be signs of enslavement to routine as much as fruit of the gospel's freedom.

What about a third response, a deep involvement in *social action?* Is not this the way we demonstrate solid discipleship? After all, the fruit that God desires from His beloved vineyard is justice and righteousness (Isaiah 5). My parents practiced such discipleship—running an orphanage in Puerto Rico, ministering to Filipinos in Stockton, pastoring the poor and underprivileged in Oakland.

That legacy has both enriched my understanding of the faith and equipped me to work for justice in my own community and beyond. But more is needed than a sense of justice as evidence of my understanding of the Christian faith. Many of my friends—Jewish, liberal, or unbelieving—share my concern for social righteousness and relief from oppression without being grasped by the truths that God has revealed in Christ.

Have you truly caught the meaning of the Christian faith? I can answer "yes" to that pivotal question only to the degree that I can face tragedy, suffering, and, especially, death with trust and peace.

It is just here that I find Marvin Hein's book so helpful. It does not try to stuff me with additional information, urge me to more exercises of spirituality, or press me to engagement in social problems. The author believes in all the above Christian expressions, but he knows that maturity comes as we are gripped by the gospel just at those points where all human news has turned bad. And his book is the stuff of which mature and joyous discipleship is made.

Like a Shock of Wheat is a book *profoundly biblical.* It pictures a sovereign God, who upholds our creation and governs our history; it calls us to see all our living and dying in the light of that sovereignty. Even more, the book depicts a sufficient gospel, which shouts its word of Christ's love, forgiveness, and power with enough cogency and clarity to be heard above the laments of tragedy or the sobs of grief.

These chapters are also *warmly pastoral*. They are a comforting rod and staff with which the great Shepherd encourages his faltering flock. They deal in sensible ways with real needs. The sufferers whose story Pastor Hein tells are our friends and neighbors. We identify with their anguish, share their losses, and empathize with their grief. Out of intimate ministry to them, he has gained the perspective to minister to us.

The viewpoint of the book is *soundly practical*. Bereavement is never far away from any of us. As the years roll on, we spend increased amounts of time in personal grief or in fellowship with those who grieve. Whatever form death takes and whenever it intrudes, the shock is massive, the trauma immense. Pat answers fade, clichés crumble, and trite suggestions evaporate. We have been outraged by life's most menacing reality, and we need incomparable support. Numb, staggered, shaken by death, we have to know its limits; we long for word of its conquest; we hanker for news of what lies beyond it; we beg for assurance that God is still there. All of these pushingly practical needs are spoken to in these pages. Time lovingly spent in them will enhance our knowledge of Christ's lordship. And nothing in the world can help us deal with death better than that.

The style of Hein's work is *skillfully artful*. The chapters teem with illustrations which warrant borrowing. History, drama, literature, and personal experience have all been quarried for the gems that brighten the theological teaching. A number of helpful poems and stanzas of verse are included to make *Like a Shock of Wheat* a sourcebook for materials to be used at funerals and in other settings needing condolence. And the writer's own sentences are alive with phrases both poignant and picturesque. It is a graceful book—both in content and form.

Have you truly caught the meaning of the Christian faith? Who would dare give an unequivocal "Aye" to that query? All of us are learners, pilgrims on the way to biblical maturity.

For such learners—whether pastors, chaplains, doctors and nurses, students planning for ministry, or patients facing death—this book was written. With it, our learning will increase. We will grasp the meaning of what we believe with firm reassurance. Or better, we will be grasped by the truths of Christ's sovereignty as a kernel of wheat is grasped by the nurturing sod. And the harvest of spiritual growth will fulfill the divine mathematics—forty, sixty, and a hundredfold.

David Allan Hubbard, President
Fuller Theological Seminary

Author's Preface

One of the most meaningful facets of a two-decade ministry in the same congregation has come in connection with death-experiences. I have walked into a hospital room and accidentally, but perhaps providentially, witnessed the homegoing of an all-alone patient. I have stood at hospital bedsides with families and watched their loved ones die. I have groaned inwardly with family members as they stood helplessly watching the all-too-slow death of someone they loved. I have tried to calm the troubled hearts of people whose dearest ones were taken in a moment from apparently good health to sudden death.

Ministering to some three hundred families through the suffering-death-bereavement experience has forced me to go to the Bible for strength and comfort—for others and for myself. I have found the greatest inspiration for preaching coming in those difficult moments of death and life. I have discovered that people's hearts are most open to reflections from the Word during such experiences. The Word speaks with freshness and appropriateness at such times of need. I have learned that the way one looks at death influences strongly one's approach to life.

Repeated confrontations with death experiences have convinced me that often we approach death with unbiblical, unrealistic attitudes and smooth, easy answers to questions that may not have satisfactory solutions. Our pastoral attempts to comfort, like the theologically inaccurate poetry to which we so often resort at memorial services, are not consistent with reality nor the Bible's views on death and life. And yet the Bible is replete with hints and suggestions about God's view of death and life.

Like a Shock of Wheat represents a pastoral theology of death. It has arisen out of direct confrontation with death in the day-to-day life of the church family. The chapters of this book do not offer a set of easy answers to suffering and death, but I hope they present a biblical approach to the human dilemmas involved in facing evil and death. Each chapter suggests a biblical response to an actual, true-to-life encounter with sorrow or death. The convictions grew out of close, intimate relationships with the dying and/or their family members. In most instances the seed-thoughts for the respective chapters incubated in my mind as I prepared funeral meditations for members of my church.

This book attempts to look at death from God's view while, at the same time, not avoiding any of the human feelings present at such times of stress. The reflections arise from the most tragic accidental deaths of the young, as well as from the struggles of the aged and infirm. The reader will find here the suggested biblical response to the gift of extended life, as well as to the unexplainable puzzle of self-destruction.

In the chapters which follow, I attempt (1) to interpret the biblical view of suffering—its origins, effects, and purposes in God's plan; (2) to express the biblical view of how to live here and now the life eternal that is available to Christian believers; and (3) to deal with the believer's hope for a heaven to be gained and a hell to be shunned.

The responses of the families with whom I have lived through the struggles and defeats and victories of death have motivated me to write this book. I owe a great debt to the members of the Hillsboro, Kansas, Mennonite Brethren congregation with whom I have worked for more than twenty years. Their constant and repeated encouragements to put into print my interpretations of the biblical views of death and life have made this book a reality. To Wally Kroeker— editor, churchman, and friend—I say a hearty "thank you" for his Barnabas-like spirit of encouragement both before and during the writing of this book. Paul M. Schrock, Herald Press Book Editor, and Katie Funk Wiebe have been most helpful in suggesting writing styles.

I gratefully acknowledge the encouragement and indulgence of my fellow workers, David D. Clark and Nadine Friesen, who must often have pondered the sanity of their "boss" as he sat silently at the typewriter searching for the right word or phrase. To Amanda Ewert, my secretary, I express my thanks for typing the manuscript during extra hours she might well have used doing other things.

Finally, I pay tribute to my wife and daughter, Mary Helen and Holly, who listened to my agonizings during the period of writing. Without complaint they surrendered the companionship of husband and father on "days off" and late night hours that I usually spend with them.

I am no doubt indebted to many others. My prayer is simply that readers of this book will sense the heartthrob of a God who knows all our feelings and infirmities and wishes to strengthen and comfort us through his eternal Word.

Marvin Hein
Fresno, California

Like a Shock of Wheat

1

Like a Shock of Wheat

Job, subject to the taunts of Satan and the doubts of his own heart, became very discouraged one day. He became critical and suspicious about the way God was treating him. He was writhing miserably in his deteriorating health. Those who once recognized him as a man of means and reputation sat in judgment upon him. In his grief and pain, Job was forced to listen to the advice of friends who now seemed to be his enemies. Most of what they said was difficult to accept because Job knew their caustic remarks were untrue.

Of Job's three friends who first spoke to him, Eliphaz undoubtedly was the most attractive. He was obviously a gentleman, sympathetic and courteous. In one of his speeches he said to suffering Job: "You shall come to your grave in ripe old age, as a shock of wheat comes up to the threshing floor in its season" (Job 5:26, RSV).

The prediction, difficult as it appeared at the moment, was nevertheless fulfilled. In the last verse of the Book of Job we read: "And Job died, an old man and full of days" (Job 42:17, NAS).

I have watched the twentieth-century Middle Eastern farmer tie his grain in bundles. I have seen the oxen treading on the straw on the threshing floor, beating out the kernels of grain. The wheat is flailed and tossed into the air so that chaff and straw are separated from the wheat. Having witnessed this primitive procedure, the words of Job's friend fascinate me. Like a shock of wheat. . . .

Recently my wife and I were called back to my birthplace for her father's memorial service. He failed by a few days to reach the ripe old age of 92. A few weeks previously the family had celebrated our parents' seventieth wedding anniversary. "Pop" and "Mom" had been well enough to enjoy the occasion with us. They were mentally alert as they and we gave thanks to God for His mercies over such a long period of time. But on this particular evening we sat around a table planning the memorial service. As an in-law I was judiciously staying out of the discussion. The children planned their father's funeral service to be an act of praise and worship. When the matter of the meditation at the service was broached, my sisters-in-law informed me that this decision had already been made. The son-in-law would preach.

I had left home hundreds of miles away without any thoughts of such an assignment. My trusty library of books and a file of sermons from more than twenty years of preaching were not readily available. I contemplated this unexpected and newly given task. I began to reflect more seriously upon the life of my aged father-in-law. He was, indeed, an old man, but very alert until shortly before his death. Longevity was characteristic of this family. An older brother was 94 years old, and a sister had passed the century mark and was still alert.

My father-in-law had been a farmer all his life. He had worked with wheat over a span of nearly 90 years. His family moved to a new homestead in Oklahoma when he was seven years old. He and his brothers walked 200 miles behind the horses and wagon that carried his mother and sisters and all their earthly possessions.

Their life in this newly claimed portion of the Cherokee Strip began on virgin soil. The tall prairie grass had to be turned over. The newly broken sod became the seedbed for the first wheat crop ever raised on that pioneer farm.

Years later, after he was married and they had one daughter, the family made another pioneer move. This time their trek took them to the more arid, unbroken prairies of western Oklahoma. Once again the sulky plow turned the grassy plains of untried but rich soil into a fertile seedbed for a harvest of golden wheat. A major part of my father-in-law's long and fruitful life revolved around the production of wheat.

In the midst of my reflections came the words of Eliphaz: "You shall come to your grave in ripe old age, as a shock of wheat comes up to the threshing floor in its season" (Job 5:26, RSV).

On many occasions I have reflected on life and death, and God's care of us in every situation of life. The longer I reflect on our Lord's view of life, advancing age, death, and what He has prepared for us, the more appropriate the symbol of the shock of wheat becomes.

Wheat Has Precarious Beginnings

When the farmer plants wheat in the fall (or in the spring in some sections of the country), he does so under a variety of conditions. Sometimes the soil has received plentiful moisture and lies prepared. The beautiful, mellow seedbed asks to receive the fragile little kernel of wheat that must die in order to give life.

Ideal conditions do not always exist, however, in those areas where wheat is produced in most abundance. When moisture is not in abundance, the soil remains rough and un-receptive to the tiny kernels of grain. When weeds or volunteer wheat have not been destroyed because of drought, the wheat can only be deposited in a polluted, competitive environment. When the soil is cloddy and rough, the farmer cannot be certain of healthy little green sprouts of wheat. Ripened grain certainly cannot be assured at planting time. When you think about the beginnings of that shock of wheat, a kind of precariousness exists that is frightening.

People are born and mature spiritually with a similar precariousness. For some the seedbed of home and church is such that it becomes a most normal experience to accept Jesus Christ as Savior and Lord. It proved to be that for my father-in-law. In checking the church records after his death, we discovered that he and three brothers and one sister were baptized on the same day. They had, as children, learned the ways of God, both by precept and example. The fertile soil of their church and family life had resulted in a good, early harvest.

Sometimes, however, even when the spiritual ground lies carefully prepared, the seed takes a long time to sprout and mature into a spiritual shock of wheat. Often, even in the most religious environment, a son or daughter proves to be like a tiny, fragile kernel of wheat, lying in the cloddy, weedy soil, awaiting the fall rains that will cause it to sprout.

Sometimes there is initial growth—a commitment to Christ but a heavy spiritual snowfall is necessary to provide moisture and nitrogen to strengthen that plant. Christ may be declared Savior but our acceptance of Him as Lord may be limited. Spiritual growth is precarious.

A shock of wheat doesn't develop overnight. Months of time are involved. Periods of cold and winter, waiting and dormancy, are essential to the production of wheat. The green succulent plant wilts and suffers in the wintry cold. Spiritually, a similar mistreatment often occurs. Life under the lordship of Christ is not always one long, steady, uninterrupted period of growth. Days of coolness, some more severe than others, characterize many Christian lives. Spiritual winters, where love and trust do not overflow, invade the tender spiritual plant. Spiritual ebb and flow represents the typical life of many believers. There are springlike days when new life explodes everywhere in the spiritual life. But amidst the days of confidence and trust cold seasons of doubts and questions arise. This spiritual shock of wheat develops precariously, both in its birth and growth.

Wheat's Usefulness Is Enhanced by Suffering

Wheat endures tortuous suffering during its lifetime. Fortunately it tolerates a great deal of mistreatment. In fact, it thrives on certain kinds of suffering. Winter wheat, planted in the Indian-summer days of autumn, takes on a beautiful hue of green rows as it sprouts and grows. It continues to attain a form of maturity if the weather is favorable, but then, hit by frost, turns a dirty, brown color, and appears to be dead. The uninformed non-farmer would conclude that cruelty is the lot of those thriving blades of wheat.

The truth is that the shock of wheat can never become a reality without the mistreatment of the frost. Wheat that lingers in the ground without sprouting until spring, when the gentle rains fall, brings no harvest. Wheat requires the trials of winter if shocks are to stand in summer.

The winter, however, is often not the end of the struggle for the wheat plant's survival and maturity. Even after the spring showers have watered the thirsty earth and the wheat has begun its revival of growth, the winds and dust make their assaults. The lush, tender leaves of what should one day result in a shock of wheat stand beaten, sometimes dashed against the ground, stripped and torn into apparent uselessness. But more often than not the wheat endures. Wheat's capacity to withstand mistreatment amazes the careful observer of this hardy perennial.

Wheat farmers know the anxieties that accompany those otherwise welcome spring thunderstorms, especially when the wheat stands nearly ripe. When the almost mature head of wheat stands proudly on the stalk, all is not safe. When the yellowish tint that holds promises of imminent harvest is present, a heavy rain and a strong wind may cause the wheat to lodge or lie down flat in the field. Or the white, billowing clouds that bring refreshing rain can also bring frozen, irregular bits of icy hail, which damage and destroy the crop in a matter of minutes. But all these experiences enter into the development of a shock of wheat.

That, too, stands as a parable for our spiritual lives and the harvest we are intended to produce. We rebel against mistreatment. We resent the pain and trial and storminess in our lives that help produce spiritual maturation. The rains fall when we would prefer sunshine. Hailstones, figuratively speaking, threaten our spiritual growth and may, indeed, harm and hinder that growth. We are tossed about. We find ourselves pressed and under stress, but such pressures constitute the ingredients of spiritual fruitfulness.

The Apostle Paul, speaking from experience and knowing full well the potential fruits of suffering, said in his epistle to the Romans: " . . . but we also exult in our tribulations, knowing that tribulation brings about perseverance; and perseverance, proven character; and proven character, hope" (Romans 5:3-4, NAS). Like a shock of wheat, the spiritual life develops in a precarious atmosphere. Repeated disturbing experiences test our spirits, but in the process we rise to levels of usefulness that would not be attained without suffering.

One cold, dark morning in the early 1900s, my father-in-law, a young man with a wife and a six-week-old daughter, experienced apparent tragedy. The family was on its way to the western Oklahoma prairies to make a new home. Traveling by horses and wagon, they were winding their way in the darkness along unpaved and rough roads. On this particular frosty morning these pioneering wheat farmers were almost frozen with fear when the wagon overturned after rumbling over a huge stone. My mother-in-law and her infant daughter were trapped beneath the overturned wagon. My father-in-law and other companions in the caravan realized that underneath the wagon was a burning stove that had provided heat for the journey. Panic and frustration prevailed until one of the travelers ripped open a canvas and helped to release the trapped family members from the overturned wagon. All were safe.

That accident and the subsequent seven consecutive years in which no wheat harvests were produced were hardly welcomed. But the suffering endured in those and other ways resulted in spiritual fruit. Those unwelcome trials played a major role in making it possible for "Pop" to sing the songs of faith in his dying days as doctors and nurses looked on in amazement at this "shock of wheat" living out its earthly existence.

The most useful people in the kingdom of God are not isolated saints protected from the ills of life. The shock of wheat that comes to a full age endures a lot of stress. The raw winter winds and the dashing rains of springtime all combine to shape the development of the character that possesses mature children of God. Tribulation is an ingredient in bringing the shock of wheat into production and usefulness.

Wheat Symbolizes Success, Not Failure

Job's friend used very descriptive language in explaining what old age is like—"as a shock of wheat comes up to the threshing floor in its season" (Job 5:26, RSV). That is death. Normally we view the departure of our loved ones as defeat, disgrace, capitulation, and failure. The Bible, on the other hand, perceives death for the believing child of God not as a crop failure but as the beginning of harvest.

Modern methods of harvesting rob us of the picture the Bible poses as to the reality of death. Combines and custom-cutting crews garnering in the golden grain over hundreds of acres in a few hours obscure for us the imagery of Eliphaz's words. The ancient Palestinian worked with very small parcels of wheat planted on stony ground and producing comparatively little grain. Threshing time represented a high moment in his life. Every bundle of wheat was important. Every kernel counted. Carefully he gathered the flailed and winnowed grain into sacks. Wheat meant sustenance and life. Harvest was a most meaningful moment in his life.

The Bible says, in essence: "Yes, you will come to your grave in ripe old age, but it will be like a shock of wheat comes up to the threshing floor in its season." That's not intended to be bad news. That's good news! Death for the believer can be likened to precious harvest for that ancient farmer who saw every kernel and bundle as the means of new life. For his family—often an extended family—that newly harvested grain supplied them with their one most staple food—bread. In that sense wheat symbolized life to them. Harvest was a crowning moment in the year. It made life possible for the rest of the year.

In the biblical sense death represents that for the Christian. It is harvesttime. It is a crowning moment—the time when life really begins to take on completely new dimensions. Death signifies homecoming. It suggests a time of celebration. It means relief from pain and suffering. It is not an end, but rather a beginning, a glorious time of victory and harvest.

I imagine the ancient Jewish farmer could have looked at those bundles of wheat and felt very sad about them. He could have recalled how, a few months ago, those beautiful green stalks of wheat decorated the landscape of his small acreage. After all, green is beautiful in the farmer's eyes. He could have wished his wheat field would remain green forever.

He could have sighed with regret when the summer sun and the hot winds caused that lush green to turn to a golden but dying brown. He could have said, "My wheat is dying." And he would have been correct. He could have hesitated there on the threshing floor and said, "But why should I abuse these heads of wheat by whipping and beating them on the ground after I have so tenderly and lovingly raised them? How ungrateful of me to mistreat these once beautiful heads of wheat?"

I'm confident the farmer didn't see it that way. He saw the non-green, apparently dead stalk of wheat as LIFE. This precious grain would sustain him and his family through the next months. As we reflect on God's view of death and life, can we see death for the believer as the biblical writer saw it?

Oh, yes, we, too, long for the green years—when things go
well and flourish. Then comes defeat and death. But from a
biblical perspective, death is victory, not defeat.

Like the farmer who flails away at that bundle of dead
straw because life has been surrendered, we look sadly at
death. But in our hearts we know death ushers us into
abundant, joyous life. God, seeing death in its real essence,
does not ask us to enjoy the homegoing of our loved ones.
He knows the hurt and pain of parting and separation. He
does not castigate us because of our tears. But He continues
to remind us that, as seen through His eyes, death is like a
shock of wheat. Death is the path to life. Death means
harvesttime. Death ushers in victory.

2

Precious Treasures in Earthen Vessels

For five years a wood treatment firm in London, England, displayed three old pieces of wood as an advertisement for their business. The company showed the battered pieces of wood as a way of saying to passersby: "Don't let this happen to your house." The firm recently went bankrupt. The wood fragments, thrown into the garbage can, remained right there because London garbage collecters were on strike. But a sharp-eyed passerby spotted the three pieces of wood, and shortly thereafter the rescued trash was sold at an auction for $21,000. When the three pieces were joined together, they proved to form a panel carved almost 500 years ago in the Low Countries of Europe showing a famous man, St. Hubert, at prayer. Precious treasure rescued from a garbage can!

When the Apostle Paul reflected on death and life, he visualized believers carrying in their bodies the beauty of Christ. He gloried in the promise that day by day that image of the risen Christ becomes more perfect in our lives. But in his second letter to the Corinthians, he portrays the sparkling contrast between the glory possible and the poor vessels in which the glory is held. "But we have this treasure in earthen vessels, that the surpassing greatness of the power may be of God and not from ourselves" (2 Corinthians 4:7, NAS).

While writing this book I was preaching through Paul's second letter to the Corinthian church. When I came to the section from which the above passage is found, the preceding week had been one of those all-too-typical times when sadness and death hang heavy over a pastor's life. A friend had committed suicide that week. A parishioner had been rushed to the hospital after suffering a stroke. A hospital patient with a broken leg learned she needed major surgery for a completely unrelated illness, in addition to the two cataracts that had already dimmed the vision in her eyes. And strangely enough, during the morning worship service a woman in the local hospital died—one with whom I had visited freely and lucidly only two days before.

The "earthiness' of the vessel—the human body—in which the glory of Christ's image resides became very real. Driven by the events of the week, together with the fact that the passage was waiting to be explained, I reflected more intently on death and life. The thought of clay pots—earthen vessels—gripped my mind as I pondered the fragile nature of the body that contains the precious treasure of God's glory. Precious treasure in earthen vessels!

Harold Begbie's book *Broken Earthenware* tells the stories of twice-born men and women. I reflected on the aptness of that title. People who have been born anew, redeemed from sin, possess a priceless treasure. But how fragile the containers of those treasures!

We Carry Christ's Death

The apostle declares that he is "always carrying about in
the body the dying of Jesus" (2 Corinthians 4:10, NAS). He
apparently refers to the indignities Jesus suffered because
His human body felt the effects of pain and death. The di-
vinity of Christ resided in an earthly body. Precious treasure
in an earthen vessel! And, we carry that death in us as well.

As I meditated over that passage, I recalled vividly a
purchase I made on my first trip abroad in 1965. Walking
into a little shop obviously arranged for tourists as
uninitiated as I, a young woman in downtown Athens sold
me several beautiful vases. They were hand-painted and
ornately decorated, and I visualized them as beautiful gifts
for my wife. I could almost see them sitting on the mantle
back in Kansas and serving as conversation pieces for years
to come. I bought them and accepted the young woman's
kind offer to ship them to America so I would not be burdened with them for the next nine weeks of travel.

Upon my return home two months later, I eagerly
awaited the arrival of my precious Greek vases. One day
they were delivered by the postman and joy abounded—
until I discovered the condition of the once-beautiful vases.
One was lying in more than a dozen pieces and the other
was badly damaged. We still treasure them, but without
Elmer's glue they would have remained in shambles.
Earthen vessels are not very sturdy.

In Paul's world, earthen vessels—small pottery lamps—
often served as the light-holders in a home. At other times,
priceless treasures were hidden in simple earthenware vases.
And in many Roman triumphal processions a customary
practice called for gold and silver to be carried in clay pots.

The longer I mused over the words of the apostle and remembered how my beautiful vases had arrived almost in

shambles, the more I reflected on the truth of the biblical view of life and death. We hold the most precious light in the world, but the containers—our bodies—are earthen jars, undependable and easily damaged. We carry death in us.

Paul vividly describes the fragile nature of this vessel. He speaks about being "handicapped on all sides ... puzzled ... persecuted ... knocked down" (2 Corinthians 4:8-9, JBP). The note of brokenness and death permeates the entire passage: "Always carrying about in our bodies the dying of Jesus ... for we who live are constantly being delivered over to death ... so death works in us ... though our outer man is decaying" (2 Corinthians 4:10, 11, 12, 16, NAS).

What a pessimistic view of the human predicament! That obvious weakness must have motivated the unbeliever, H. G. Wells, to write: "Mankind is not the privileged favorite of Mother Nature and in spite of all my lifelong optimism, it now seems to me that the whole universe is utterly bored by the whole species of mankind." Wells viewed the human race as being swept along to degradation and utter extinction. Viewing only the fragile container in which the beautiful light dwells, such pessimism comes rather easily.

Another story portrays graphically that note of pessimism. A man planned to jump off the Brooklyn Bridge to end his life. The precipitous fall was averted when a policeman grabbed him just as he prepared to leap. An animated conversation followed. The depressed, suicidal man showed the policeman the morning newspaper—then both men jumped off the bridge.

Watching the human body deteriorate can well lead to such an attitude. To gaze day after day upon a degenerating earthen vessel on a sickbed doesn't always motivate the highest thoughts. We may begin to think like Thomas Hood:

> I remember, I remember
> The fir-trees dark and high.
> I used to think their slender tops
> Were close against the sky.
> It was a childish ignorance
> But now 'tis little joy
> To know I'm farther off from heaven
> Than when I was a boy.

I suppose Hood felt like the boy who has just conquered algebra, only to discover that calculus is a vast unknown. If we think only of the fragile, earthenware vessel that is our body, we may well feel despondent. The bad news is that we carry death in us. But good news awaits us.

We Carry Christ's Life

The child whose elementary skills in arithmetic suddenly appear so inadequate and weak upon encountering the complexities of trigonometry, nevertheless already holds the key to further conquests. In the same way, the child of God with an earthen vessel as his body, nevertheless possesses a glory that cannot be compared with any other treasure. For that reason the apostle insisted that while he was knocked down, he never suffered a knockout. He endured persecution but he never experienced forsakenness.

Just as the passage in 2 Corinthians is punctuated with our weakness or earthiness, just so we discover words about our life in Jesus Christ in the same verses. Paul speaks of being "raised [with] the Lord Jesus" (2 Corinthians 4:14, NAS), and he refers to something experienced in this life. Once again, after reminding us that our outward body decays, he reassures us by stating that "our inner man is being renewed day by day" (2 Corinthians 4:16, NAS), and again this represents a process going on in this present life. Finally, when speaking of affliction, which he considers "light," he proceeds to interpret that suffering as "producing for us an eternal weight of glory far beyond all comparison" (2 Corinthians 4:17, NAS).

The reminder about possessing the treasure in an earthen vessel compels us to remember that we cannot take credit for anything. Our fragile bodies remind us of that repeatedly. But the picture of renewal and growing glory leaves no room for wallowing in despair. In fact, the brokenness makes possible the development of this priceless treasure. We bear our afflictions willingly, if we follow the biblical view of life, because we know that through them we move from glory to glory.

Many years ago the Hoover Dam project brought fertility and fruitfulness to thousands of acres of desert land. In the process of construction, some men lost their lives in accidents and disasters. When the dam was completed a plaque was placed into the wall of this huge concrete structure. Inscribed on the plaque were the names of the workmen who had died. Below the men's names these words were inscribed: "These died that the desert might rejoice and blossom as the rose."

Following the biblical view of death and life, such a process continues in the believer's life constantly. We carry death in us so that life can issue out from us. The student struggles to learn long division and algebra (even though he thinks it will kill him) so that trigonometry and calculus can be conquered later. The struggle in the earthen vessel enables the child of God to possess an eternal weight of glory.

Salomon De La Silva wrote a poem entitled "Measure." In it she asked herself whether the water in a pool should be best measured by the earth that holds the water, or by the heaven the water holds. She then proceeds to ask the same question about life. Should man be measured by the earthen vessel in which his glory is encased, or by the heaven the frail human body contains?

The biblical view is that glory abounds in humans. Suffering and death assist in producing that glory. The earthen vessel takes a beating so that the spiritual life can grow. In darkness and trials the light grows. Some things we never possess unless we experience the darkness. Some glories never become ours unless we have walked through the gloom. The wear and tear of the body, real as it is, provides the background against which the inward man receives renewed strength.

The daffodils of spring push their way through the ground after a hard cold winter. The springtime flowers and shrubs and trees burst with greenery because chlorophyll, a miraculous sun-trap, transforms the sun's light into energy for rebuilding. In the spirit-life God provides for a "sun-trap" that, in spite of the wintry-like suffering imposed on the earthen vessel, brings renewal and glory.

Recently I visited with a man in my congregation who has suffered intensely from rheumatoid arthritis. Complications have included a blood clot in his leg and emphysema in his lungs. He shared frankly about some of his discouraging days. But he also told of a good day he recently enjoyed. After reading an encouraging letter from a friend in California, he reached for the devotional book, *Streams in the Desert*. That day's reading contained these lines:

> No, chance hath brought this ill to me;
> 'Tis God's own hand, so let it be,
> He seeth what I cannot see.
> There is a need-be for each pain,
> And He one day will make it plain
> That earthly loss is heavenly gain.
> Like as a piece of tapestry

Viewed from the back appears to be
Naught but threads tangled hoplessly;
But in the front a picture fair
Rewards the worker for his care,
Proving his skill and patience rare.
Thou art the Workman, I the frame.
Lord, for the glory of Thy Name,
Perfect Thine image on the same.

What a beautiful picture of what Paul expressed in his letter to the church in Corinth! Precious treasuse in an earthen
vessel! My friend's suffering would appear to many to be
wasted energy. But Bill endures the pain and remains coura-
geous in spite of great odds because he recognizes God is
making a beautiful piece of tapestry out of his life.

As his friends, we see only the back side—where all the
knots and stray ends appear—and the picture appears
unsightly. It hurts to see him suffer. But if we could see the
front, as God views the scene, we would see the picture fair.
And so my friend, hurting but confident in God's good work,
says with the poet:

Thou art the Workman, I the frame.
Lord, for the glory of thy Name,
Perfect Thine image on the same.

God gives us earthen vesels. We carry in us the death of
Jesus. But precarious as those lamps of clay prove to be, they
contain a precious treasure. Like rescuing junky pieces of
wood from the garbage heap and finding them worth thousands of dollars, God works through our frail bodies and our
sometimes impatient suffering—to work out a glorious picture. We become more and more the image of Jesus Christ.

3

Light Shining Out of Darkness

I resist evading the reality of death. I recoil inwardly when people downplay the hurt of separation through death. I resent acting as if death holds no fears. Experience, though usually vicarious, teaches me that death strikes terror into many hearts. I have sometimes considered it cruel to subject mourning relatives and friends to some of the poetry used at funerals.

> There is no death—
> They only truly live
> Who pass into the life beyond, and see
> This earth is but a school preparative
> For larger ministry.

I appreciate the author John Oxenham, and recognize that his elequent lines possess a character and a theology that surpasses many. And there is some truth in the above stanza, but have you sat with a grieving widow and tried to

tell her there is no death? Death is real. Death is darkness.
Death is rude—especially when you are the one most closely
affected.

George Washington Bethune wrote words that express
biblical truth about death:

> It is not death to die,
>   To leave this weary road,
> And, midst the brotherhood on high,
>   To be at home with God.

Intellectually I accept those words. But when I sit beside
the emaciated body of a terminally ill friend, the words
sound cold: "It is not death to die." I want to shout back at
the poet: "It is terrible to die." Death is darkness. Death is
intensely real.

Some unknown author wrote:

> What is death? A little broadening of a ripple
> Upon the eternal shore.
> A little loosening of the bands that cripple—
> This and nothing more.

Have you ever tried those lines on a weeping, questioning
woman who was robbed of speaking some much-needed last
words to her husband when he slumped over in the living
room dead? I do not doubt the truth of the poet's words. I
only insist that for the sufferer death is terribly real. Separation frightens and incapacitates.

> I cannot say, and I will not say
> That he is dead. He is just away!

> With a cheery smile, and a wave of the hand,
> He has wandered into an unknown land.

Beautiful words! Congratulations, James Whitcomb

Riley, for giving them to us. But their pleasant sentiments (true as they may be) sound like mockery when I counsel with a bereaved person who, after six months, insists the pain of separation multiplies rather than diminishes. Darkness engulfs the bereaved in many instances. Nor does the presence of darkness necessarily imply lack of spirituality.

In reflecting upon death and life, I have been forced to accept the harshness and rudeness of death. That my reflection is biblical to some degree is substantiated by what I read in 2 Corinthians: "For God, who said, 'Light shall shine out of darkness,' is the One who has shone in our hearts to give the light of the knowledge of the glory of God in the face of Christ" (4:6, NAS).

Living in the Midst of Darkness

Having spoken candidly about the darkness in the wake of death, let me also say that I have watched with delight as new life appeared. I have stood in virtual unbelief as bereaved family members found light in the presence of darkness. The brightest shafts of light have sometimes come from the deepest, cavern-like experiences where you would think no light is possible.

But light exerts its influence effectively only against a background of darkness. Without darkness light changes nothing appreciably. The Apostle Paul, when he wrote the passage quoted above, may have been pondering the words of Isaiah: "The people who walked in darkness have seen a great light; those who dwelt in a land of deep darkness, on them has light shined" (Isaiah 9:2, RSV).

Light is most apparent in the presence of darkness. Darkness accentuates the light. So Paul said, "Let light shine out of darkness" (2 Corinthians 4:6b, RSV). Living creatively and realistically implies the acceptance of an arena for living that contains darkness. That's the way life is lived—against a background of darkness. Futile are the efforts to imagine that life consists of living perpetually in the light.

The gospel is the good news hurled into a setting of bad news. Salvation intrudes only where lostness exists. The story of Bethlehem and the birth of Jesus is couched in a dark setting. Jesus' birth merited attention because it was light shining out of darkness. Even the physical surroundings of His birth provided a dim, unwelcome setting for the Christ-event. But the darkness of the Judean night enabled the wise men to discover the star. Light out of darkness!

Our culture confuses us by insisting that answers lie ready at hand for every situation. The church often adds to that confusion by suggesting that faithful discipleship assures the absence of darkness. That is misleading. We live against a background of darkness. Frederick Beuchner said:

> . . . we are also, God knows, a people who walk in darkness. If darkness is meant to suggest a world where nobody can see very well—either themselves, or each other, or where they are heading, or even where they are standing at the moment; if darkness is meant to convey a sense of uncertainty of being lost, of being afraid; if darkness suggests conflict, conflict between races, between nations, between individuals each pretty much out for himself when you come right down to it; then we live in a world that knows much about darkness.

The real world in which people suffer and die contains loads of darkness. Reflecting upon death and life necessitates dealing with darkness. Beuchner has gone on to suggest that if we are praying people, darkness probably motivates much of that praying. And if we are not praying persons, darkness in one form or another probably stops our mouths.

I am simply appealing for a realistic attitude that includes darkness as a key ingredient in life. The Bible portrays life honestly. It never hides the darkness that invades our lives. Jesus openly and wisely prepared His followers by suggesting that they would experience tribulation (darkness) in the world.

Our Lord discovered very quickly in His earthly life that His activities would be carried out against a background of darkness and intrigue. He prayed in Gethsemane because He faced the reality of being separated from the Father. He cried out on the cross when that separation occurred. Even He could not escape the maddening darkness against which most of life is lived. Dare we expect less darkness than He? But because of the darkness, God in Christ appeared. Because of that darkness, the apostle called for light to shine out of darkness. One more light shining out of what is already light doesn't make much of a splash. Light affects us most when it beams out of darkness.

Living in the Face of Glory

If the Bible honestly portrays a dark world, it also candidly depicts the believer's life as one capable of being full of light. God is the One who has shined in our hearts. His Son entered the human dilemma to give light—the light of the glory of God. Life consists not only of darkness. Life in Jesus Christ reverberates with joy and light.

In another chapter I refer to the Hebrew exile as their Gethsemane. Through the decades of slavery the prayer rose daily: "Let this cup pass from me." Few of those Israelites realized they were the instruments through which the world's redemption would be effected. What remained darkness for them became the rich spiritual deposit from which was drawn the Redeemer of the world. The light of the world, Jesus Christ, had His roots in those people of God.

Living in the face of glory became a possibility when the

world was blanketed with darkness. The cross-experience contained a space of time when the earth shook—in darkness. Darkness preceded the dawning of new life and light in the world. What glory has exploded in Jesus Christ against that background of heaviness and gloom!

Living in the face of glory becomes the experience of many who face deep sadness. "Weeping may last for the night, but a shout of joy comes in the morning" (Psalm 30:5b, NAS), affirmed the psalmist. The glory of God in the face of Jesus Christ revolutionizes life and turns darkness into light. A Joni Eareckson loses the use of her arms and legs, but discovers the glory of God in the face of Jesus Christ. A Merrill Womack suffers grotesque burns in an airplane crash, but struggles through darkness into the glory of God in the face of Jesus Christ.

Some of the most beautiful people in the world are the products of deep sorrow. Some of the most exhilarating experiences of my pastoral ministry have come through the lives of people who have walked through the valley of the shadow of death. Darkness and deep sorrow, only accentuate the glory now resident in their life and witness.

Who was this man of God who reminded us that light should shine out of darkness? If we were to continue reading in 2 Corinthians 4, we would soon discover he was not speaking as a theoretician. He was Exhibit A of the glory and the light possible in Jesus Christ. He testified that he was afflicted, but not crushed; perplexed but not despairing; persecuted, but not let down; struck down, but not annihilated. The Apostle Paul experienced both the darkness and the light.

Vast amounts of darkness can be endured when we live in the hope of the glory of God. Four people were asked to participate in a panel discussion in a black church many years ago. One of the participants was Clarence Darrow, the famous attorney and skeptic of the church. The depths of the Depression had embittered many. Money and jobs were scarce, and morale dipped to new lows. Clarence Darrow capitalized on that predicament to point out the plight of the black people. But in summing up their woes he said: "And yet you sing! No one can sing like you do! What do you have to sing about?" As quick as a flash a lady in the congregation shouted: "We've got Jesus to sing about!" And for once Clarence Darrow found himself without words.

The eloquent debater met face to face with someone who believed that weeping may endure for a time, but joy will come in the morning. He encountered a people who had discovered and were demonstrating the glory of God in the face of Jesus Christ.

We meet the glory of God in the face of Jesus Christ. One of our primary tasks as believers is to keep the wonder of the glory of God in the face of Christ. One of the risks of life is to allow that wonder to fade into the light of common day. When that awe and wonder slip out of our lives, the glory is lost in the gray of plodding days. When we lose the light of the knowledge of the glory of God in the face of Christ, a withering blight of the soul sets in.

Joni Eareckson, referred to earlier, expressed so beautifully how glory and light rises out of darkness: "That's just what God did for me when He sent a broken neck my way. He blew out the lamps in my life which lit up the here and now and made it so exciting. The dark despair which followed wasn't much fun. But it sure did make what the Bible says about heaven come alive. One day, when Jesus comes back, God is going to throw open heaven's shutters. And there's not a doubt in my mind that I'll be fantastically more excited and ready for it than if I were on *my feet.* You see, suffering gets us ready for heaven." °

Light shining out of darkness! That's what has happened to the quadriplegic, confined to a wheelchair. A dive into Chesapeake Bay broke her neck. Darkness surrounded her whole being. But God has sent light—for her and for the thousands who read her books and listen to her testimonies.

We tend to believe we must wait for heaven to discover the glories that rise from the dust and ashes of suffering. But the glory comes in this life, too. Joni says it well on the back cover of her second book: "Today as I look back, I am convinced that the whole ordeal of my paralysis was inspired by God's love. I wasn't the brunt of some cruel divine joke. God had reasons behind my suffering, and learning some of them has made all the difference in the world."

° Joni Eareckson and Steve Estes, *A Step Further* (Grand Rapids: Zondervan, 1978), p. 179.

4

How Will We Ever Make It?

Standing on a ladder, he was repairing the roof of their farmhouse. He lost his footing and fell to the ground. The resulting jolt damaged his vertebrae and spinal cord. After several days in traction in a hospital bed, Irvin died. Upon examining his Bible after his death, I found what the family said had been his favorite psalm. Carefully I read the words. "How could he let your foot stumble? How could he, your guardian, sleep" (Psalm 121:3, NEB)?

How ironic! A man who fell to his death treasured the psalm that assured him: "The Lord will guard you against all evil; he will guard you, body and soul" (Psalm 121:7, NEB). Incapacitating and fatal accidents prove, for some people, that the Bible blatantly states untruths. God allowed this man's foot to stumble. The guardian angel slept when he was needed most. Perhaps his soul was kept from evil, but certainly not his body.

The psalmist spoke these words to men and women who

sensed the need of God's protective custody over their lives.
At least once in a lifetime every male Jew felt constrained to
journey to Jerusalem for feast-days. Many made the trip
often. Hazards abounded on that trek. Thieves and robbers,
knowing the times when visitors traveled to the Holy City,
waited along the way to ambush the pilgrims. The midday
sun and the desert sands added to the precariousness of the
journeys.

Travelers to the sacred city needed the assurance of these
words: "The guardian of Israel never slumbers, never sleeps.
The Lord is your guardian, your defence at your right hand;
the sun will not strike you by day nor the moon by night.
The Lord will guard you against all evil; he will guard you,
body and soul" (Psalm 121:3-7, NEB).

Admittedly the Old Testament people of God associated
God's presence and blessing with physical protection and
prosperity more than we do. The New Testament clearly
teaches us that Christian discipleship excuses no one from
the hazards of pneumonia, heart attacks, or arteriosclerosis.
The fact remains, however, that the psalmist vividly portrays
the contrasting ways God and man reflect upon death and
life. The literalness with which the Hebrew writer spoke
may not be acceptable to us; the essential truth of his
message, nevertheless, remains as applicable today as ever.

Man Sees Danger; God Sees Deliverance

Imagine a typical traveling party of Hebrews sitting
around the evening campfire. Perhaps they had already encountered and skirmished with a marauding band of robbers
during the day. No doubt reports of other hazards and previous sad experiences reached their ears from time to time.
As they warmed themselves around the fire, fear and terror
gripped the hearts of the more timid. I can imagine them

speaking to each other: "How will we ever make it? Roads infested with robbers. Insufficient water to cross the arid desert. Elderly pilgrims unable to withstand the pitiless glare of the sun. And those eternal hills—one range after the other—how will we ever make it?"

But the brave souls in the festival-bound party confidently believed God's protection and their own preparedness would combine to afford safety. Where one person saw danger, another sensed deliverance. One saw the steep mountain paths to be traversed; the other trusted in God's renewing strength. One thought only of robbers; the other took notice of the night watchmen stationed at the top of strategic neighboring hills to warn of possible dangers.

The psalmist represents the confident pilgrim. He saw a God who neither slumbers nor sleeps. He perceived the Lord's protection as more effective than a human sentry at his post. He saw in those hills that threatened the faint-hearted a symbol of the strength and power of the almighty God. Where the fearful soul sensed danger and hazards, the man of faith saw the strength and care of God.

But I can also imagine that more than once a group of pilgrims did not complete their journey without casualties. Perhaps they lost their traveler's checks to enterprising thieves. Perhaps an older grandfather collapsed on the desert and died. Even a younger person could contract an illness and, because no medical help was readily available, die. God didn't always literally deliver His people. Was God sleeping?

That same question perplexes many people in our day. In our town a college freshman dived into a too-shallow lake and broke several vertebrae. Today, paralyzed from the chest down, he faces a lifetime of wheelchair existence. He enrolled in college 1,500 miles from home, persuaded this was the will of God for him. That college career lasted

scarcely two weeks. Does God never slumber nor sleep? The
Lord will be your guardian, preserving *body* and soul? The
young man battled from near death to a triumphant faith.
His parents supported him admirably. His grandfather, having only recently lost a son in a Missionary Aviation Fellowship plane crash, discovered a myriad of questions arising in
his mind. Can the words of the psalmist really be trusted?

An agnostic once challenged Joseph Parker's faith. Parker,
who later became a famous preacher, was asked: "What did
Providence do for the martyr Stephen when he was being
stoned to death?" Parker responded: "What did Providence
do in the case of the martyr Stephen? He enabled Stephen
to say: 'Lord, lay not this sin to their charge.' " God did not
spare him from stoning, but He preserved him from the
spirit of hate. The Lord spared not his life, but delivered him
from the desire to retaliate.

God never promised His children immunity to trouble
and accidents and evils. But God still maintains He will deliver us from *real* harm. The ills we experience create uncomfortable, frustrating, painful situations. But even
physical death is not the ultimate evil. We tend to view
those experiences as evil; God sees them in terms of deliverance.

The day before my parishioner Irvin died, I spoke with
him in the hospital. We had learned to love each other
through difficult experiences. He had once come to thank
me for forcibly taking him to a hospital psychiatric ward
when he was deeply disturbed. As we rehearsed that
experience and others in his hospital room, I concluded by
saying: "Irvin, it's been a pretty tough life for you, hasn't
it?" Unable to move his head or hardly his mouth because of
traction apparatus, he nevertheless answered clearly, "It
could be worse."

None of us knows whether or not he sensed he was dying. But I believe he was living by the words of the psalmist. Even dying did not constitute the ultimate evil. The Lord had preserved him from the worst evil. His foot had slipped off a ladder, yes, but he saw more than danger; he saw deliverance. That is a godly attitude—where we sense danger, destruction, and annihilation, God sees strength, deliverance, and life.

Man Sees Exits; God Sees Entrances

The common doorstep held great significance for Jews in biblical times. Crossing the threshold of one's house carried with it deep religious connotations. Paul, knowing the Jewish mind, probably recalled the traditions and customs of his day when he wrote, "The Lord will guard your going and your coming, now and for evermore" (Psalm 121:8, NEB)

Even today many Jewish families hang small containers over the doorposts of their houses. In those containers lies a piece of parchment on which is inscribed the words: "Hear, O Israel, the Lord is our God, one Lord, and you must love the Lord your God with all your heart and soul and strength" (Deuteronomy 6:4-5, NEB). Upon coming in and going out of their homes, the faithful Hebrew repeated those words. The "Shema" reminded him that God served as the Protector even as He did when the blood was sprinkled over the doorposts of Israel and the death angel passed over.

Exits and entrances into homes take on more meaning today in many parts of the world than in America. In many Eastern lands no one places his foot on the threshold. It must be stepped *over*, never *on*. The combination of these interesting practices demonstrates an interesting lesson as we

reflect on God's view of death and life. The psalmist did not
say, "I will be with your coming in and going out." The
order instead consists of exit and entrance, and not the
reverse. "The Lord will guard your going and your coming
..." (Psalm 121:8, NEB). Home equals destination. The
world outside was never seen as the final point of a journey.
Home always beckoned to the faithful Jew as the ultimate
abiding place.

The Christian's view of death and life makes that same
distinction. Death is not going out. For the believer death
means coming home. We perceive death to be departing,
passing away, or making an exit. God looks at death differently. He sees His children's death as coming in. Although we view death as an exit, God sees it as entrance.
Death equals arrival, not departure.

The Lord promised to guard us in our going out. That
speaks to our life in the world. And how often He guards us
when we are completely unaware. But His promise includes
our coming in. That speaks of our entrance into the glories
and presence of Christ. In our finite view death appears as
an exit. In God's infinite look, death is arrival. Thomas
Curtis Clark captures that viewpoint in his poem "The
Journey":

> When Death, the angel of our higher dreams,
> Shall come, far ranging from the hills of light
> He will not catch me unaware; for I
> Shall be as now communing with the dawn.
> For I shall make all haste to follow him
> Along the valley, up the misty slope
> Where life lets go and Life at last is born.
> There I shall find the dreams that I have lost
> On toilsome earth, and they will guide me on,
> Beyond the mists unto the farthest height.
> I shall not grieve except to pity those
> Who cannot hear the songs that I shall hear.

The key words in those lines rest in the line "Where life lets go and Life at last is born." The writer deliberately spelled the first "life with a small "l." The life that is born at death he spelled with a capital "L."

God's view of death and life parallels that of the poet. Life here on earth, the going out, is life with a small "l." But death, the coming in, as the psalmist spoke of it, is Life with a capital "L" because it is entrance into His glories.

Even as I write these words I am informed of the tragic death of a friend in her mid-twenties. Crushed under the wheels of a locomotive, she was taken to a hospital where it became obvious she was little more than a breathing vegetable. This forenoon, when the life-support system was withdrawn, at the request of the family, she died immediately. I ask a hundred questions, as the family surely must. I find few answers. I can only trust that the psalmist wrote God-breathed words. David shared with us something of God's view of death and life. I suffer, because I am human, some of the typical grief common to those who see apparent departures from this life. But I place my trust in the God who allows life with a small "l" to be loosed so that Life with a capital "L" can be born.

I tend to see exits. God be praised that He interprets death as an entrance. I trust Him. I believe; I want Him to help me in my unbelief.

5

Death and Shadows

More than fifteen years ago I was asked to officiate at the funeral service of a man who had known darkness. Shadows had surrounded the man's life. Tragedy and sadness stalked his life like an animal hunting its prey.

Preparing for that memorial service, I read a sermon written by a pastor who was fully aware that he would soon die. He requested that his own sermon be read at his funeral. His message began this way:

I have now come to the end of the road; I am looking out on the sunshine for the last time; the darkness of the shadow of death is falling about me, even as the shadows of the evening creep upon one at the close of the day. The sun of my day is sinking in the west. As I sit in the shadow, what message have I for you who are still in the midday of sunshine and for you who are starting out in the vigor of the morning? What have I to say to you who are approaching the shadows of evening, perhaps with fear and dread? This is my message, my last word as a preacher.

Having written those words, the preacher quoted a familiar verse, "Even though I walk through the valley of the shadow of death, I fear no evil; for Thou art with me" (Psalm 23:4a, NAS). In the remainder of his final message he shared with his people thoughts about shadows.

The Holy Spirit guided the psalmist to speak of death as walking through shadows. I have reflected on that symbolism often when witnessing the struggles of the dying. Shadows may be fleeting, but sometimes they roll into months and years. When we live under those darkening clouds, the picture of death as a shadow proivdes substance for reflection upon death and life.

At least 18 times the Bible refers to death as a shadow. The psalmist talks about God satisfying the hungry soul and filling "those who dwelt in darkness and in the shadow of death" (Psalm 107:10a, NAS). In the same psalm the writer talks about God having brought "them out of darkness and the shadow of death" (Psalm 107:14a, NAS). The prophet Isaiah said: "The people that walked in darkness have seen a great light; they that dwelt in the land of the shadow of death, upon them hath the light shined" (Isaiah 9:2, ASV).

The biblical writers chose the picture of shadow to illustrate death. We do well to reflect on that symbolism.

Shadows Distort Reality

I do not often work in my study at night. But one night I left the office section of the church after some late study. Just as I opened the door I was frightened by an approaching figure. I reeled backward for a moment. Then I realized that the specter coming at me was my own shadow. The shadow was real, but it distorted reality. No danger threatened. The lights piercing the darkness in a unique way had raised anxious thoughts within me because a shadow was placed in my path. What I thought was present didn't actually exist.

When we face death, we do well to remember that the shadow plays tricks on the mind. We sense the possibility of death, and the accuracy of our spiritual vision is destroyed. We are beset with spiritual astigmatism. What we see isn't really the way it is. Shadows distort reality.

When death approaches, when we come close to that valley of shadows, the pathway ahead appears dark and gloomy. The shadows indicate lack of security and safety. But that's because we can't see what is really present. When facing that valley, we need to let faith remind us that the path ahead, though shrouded with shadows, is just as safe, secure, and beautiful as the way we have just traveled.

One of the hazards of shadows is that they play tricks on us. They distort the picture, for we perceive incorrect impressions. Death tells me life is not worth living when my partner dies. Death whispers that everything is lost when my closest friend dies. Death tempts me to believe that it would have been better never to possess friends than to have them and lose them. Death may even suggest that it would have been better never to have been born.

Shadows distort the truth. Shadows hide reality. Shadows persuade us of things that are not facts.

Shadows Never Harm Us

Shadows create fear, but they cannot hurt us. Shadows distort and deceive and frighten us, but shadows alone cannot harm us. Most of us know the frightening feeling of a shadow passing unexpectedly across our path. While driving a car, an airplane's shadow passes overhead and we literally duck. The shadow precipitates fear in us, but can do us no harm.

The shadow has no power to harm us unless we become alarmed by the fleeting phantom. Our fright may send the automobile into the ditch, but it is not the shadow that drives the vehicle astray. Our response, not the shadow, harms us.

Walking through the valley of the shadow of death can take firm hold on us. It can distort our thinking processes and our emotions and drive us to distraction. If it is a shadow, it hides light from us, but it never grasps us nor forces us by its own strength to act irrationally. Shadows have the potential of terrorizing us, but we need to understand they are passing and only the absence of light at the moment.

On May 19, 1780, the world witnessed a total eclipse of the sun. Many thought judgment day had arrived. At noon the skies were gray; by midafternoon there was darkness as if it were night. The Connecticut House of Representatives was in session. Some legislators went to their knees in prayer. Others asked for immediate adjournment. The Speaker of the House, Colonel Davenport, silenced the assembly with these words:

"The Day of Judgment is either here or it is not. If it is not, there is no cause for adjournment. If it is, I choose to be found doing my duty. I wish, therefore, that the candles be lighted and we proceed with our business."

For that man the shadows held no fears. They only canceled the light for a time. His response consisted of doing his duty until he knew whether or not it was reality or a passing absence of light.

Death casts its shadow upon us and we may feel like stopping everything. Impending war and conflict in the world may stifle and incapacitate our wills. Death in our families can disarm us into uselessness. But the believer remembers the words of the psalmist about death being a shadow. The shadow is incapable of hurting us. It is not the real thing.

Shadows Vanish in the Light

When you are walking in the sunlight and wish to see your shadow, in which direction do you have to look? You must look away from the source of light in order to observe your shadow. When you walk toward the light, the shadow follows you; it does not precede you. When the sun is low in the west and I walk in that direction, it casts long shadows, but they are always behind me.

When reflecting upon death we need to make certain that we keep attention focused on the light. When we live in the past, which is normal in grief, we take our eyes off the One who is the light. When we remember only the good days of the past, we rob ourselves of the light that is available for our present and future. The grief-stricken person cannot be blamed for pondering the past, but eventually victory comes only when the eyes are focused on Jesus Christ, who is the light.

Forgetting to fix our eyes on the light and dwelling on the past results in shadows plaguing our footsteps. The future darkens increasingly when we insist on living in the past. The tomorrows can be enjoyed only when we face the light of life. This light knows all the tomorrows.

Fearing no evil in the face of the shadow of death, as the psalmist said, infers that we face the light. The hymnwriter spoke of this as turning your eyes upon Jesus, looking full in His wonderful face. The consequences, the songwriter said, would be that the things of earth would grow strangely dim in the light of God's glory and grace. When you direct your attention away from the past and toward the light, the shadows remain behind. The light is ahead.

Shadows Bring Out the Beauty

Life would be dull, drab, and monotonous if it were not for the shadows of life. To the grieving or suffering soul, those words may sound cruel. Shadows, nevertheless, in spite of their dreadfulness, emphasize the beauty in the world.

The man whose life and death focused my attention on Psalm 23 was a beautiful illustration of shadows bringing out beauty. More than 35 years before his death, he literally walked through the valley of the shadow of death. The shadow's effect lingered in his life. He remained physically maimed, but the Lord enabled him to look to the light. That shadow transformed his life. He was never the same. He suffered physically, but spiritually the journey through the valley of the shadow proved to be a merciful trek. God used that winding, treacherous road to bring beauty out of his life.

The artist understands the functions of shadows. Painting a landscape scene, the artist brushes in the sky, ground, trees, grass, and other objects. Every line stands out clearly. Many of us would conclude the painting is ready for framing.

To the eye of the painter, however, the picture remains far from complete. With a wide brush he begins to stroke dark blotches which represent shadows. The fine details he first placed on the canvas are almost obliterated. The distinctness is lost in the shadows. And most of us would say: "You have ruined the picture with all those drab shadows. You should have stopped much sooner."

But the shadows we think will ruin the painting only bring out its beauty. The painting, once it includes shadows, becomes a masterpiece. Life is similar. The dark shadows we fear and dread are the touches of the Master Artist. In God's

wonderful wisdom and mercy, He brushes the shadows
across our lives. Gazed upon at close range, they appear to
be the ruination of our lives. Viewed from a longer and
wider perspective, those shadowy experiences bring out the
glory. The shadows emphasize the light.

I recall reading a book describing the life of an Amish
family. One of the daughters was to be married soon.
Several weeks prior to that happy event, the bridegroom
died. For months the young woman brooded. She silently
blamed God for this misfortune in her life. She lived under
the spell of deep, dark shadows. Life was wasted time. She
groveled in the lost past. She wished she, too, had died.
Then one day she found the grace to turn to Him who is the
light. She was transformed into a new person. All who knew
her sensed a different spirit. The grand Artist in her life had
painted in the shadows. He used those shadows to paint a
beautiful picture.

6

Haven't You
Heard?

In college my major was in history. I have forgotten many
of the dates so laboriously memorized for examinations. I recall vaguely that certain battles virtually shaped the history
of the world. The specifics of when and where the forces of
Islam spread or how Christianity became the predominate
religion of the Western world no longer dwell consciously in
my mind. I have forgotten much.

One thing I do remember. Throughout those four years of
college history, one overarching concept was drilled into my
being: God is the Lord of history. My major professor, a
lifelong student of history, never let his students forget that
central idea. Men and nations would swing their heavy
clubs, but ultimately God would order the world's affairs.
God plays second fiddle to no one.

We students sometimes tired of hearing about the Kul-
turkampf (the struggle between the Roman Catholic Church
and the German government from 1873 to 1887). But our

major professor, having written his doctoral dissertation on that subject, often referred to that struggle. He talked about Bismarck and Windthorst about whom I remember all too little. But I recall vividly the inevitable conclusion of my professor; in the affairs of men and nations, God rules.

That persuasion about the abiding sovereignty of God has strengthened me many times. A form of satisfying relaxation comes over me when I watch the international struggles in the world and remember that God is the Lord of history. But that lordship over history has implications that apply much closer to my daily life. God's sovereignty pertains not simply to the affairs of nations. His rulership is just as applicable to our personal lives.

When I stand at the bedside of a friend dying of cancer, I remember my history lesson. When I empathize with a family whose loved one has suddenly been killed in an accident, I recall what I learned in college about God's rule over history. When I question the fairness of life for me personally, or for others, I resort often to the conviction of my historical mentor: God is the Lord of history.

God's sovereignty assists me in reflecting properly about death and life. Balance returns to my mind when I am tossed about by the exasperating events of the day—if I remember that God is the Lord of history. My questions and doubts dissipate more quickly when I ponder the inscrutable ways of God and His lordship of life and history.

The Hebrew people of God often forgot that He was Lord. They were tempted to believe that God had deserted them. They often felt that God had gone on vacation or was asleep. To such a despondent and doubting people of God, Isaiah would say something akin to: "Haven't you heard? Don't you remember His words? Have you not understood how this Lord of history operates in the world?"

I need that reminder as much as did the Hebrews. I need to remember the prophet's stabbing reminder when I grapple with the human frailties and sicknesses of my people. When trouble and misfortune multiply and overwhelm the soul, it is I who need to hear the words, "Have you not heard?" It is I who need to be awakened, not God.

God Is the Ruling Lord

God doesn't publish a daily newspaper. No weekly fact sheet delivered to my breakfast table tells me about the wonderful victories of God in the past week. The nightly telecast reviews none of the interventions of God in the making of history.

But the daily newspaper does tell me how China and Iran and Saudia Arabia and the USA are fashioning the history of the world. Walter Cronkite recounts many events that would lead me to believe that someone besides God is at the controls. We tend to believe what is drilled into our ears and minds most often. It is not strange then that we are tempted to think like Hebrew children: that men and nations are simply slugging it out; there is no supervision or intervention from heaven.

The daily obituary column in the newspaper is no more kind than the evening newscast. People die for useless reasons. Men and women are killed not because they have served their period of usefulness, but because of someone's stupidity.

We know all too well who determines the world's history. The nations that threaten loudly often manipulate the rest of the world. The country that manufactures the most powerful bombs forges the course of history. The nation that can commandeer the most brilliant minds and produce the most awesome arsenal of weapons determines the future. The media tell us who is going to win.

When I am bombarded with such thoughts, I need to hear the words of the prophet:

> Are you so ignorant? Are you so deaf to the words of God—the words he gave before the worlds began? Have you never heard nor understood? It is God who sits above the circle of the earth. (The people below must seem to him like grasshoppers!) He is the one who stretches out the heavens like a curtain and makes his tent from them. He dooms the great men of the world and brings them all to naught. They hardly get started, barely take root, when he blows on them and their work withers and the wind carries them off like straw. Isaiah 40:21-24, LB.

Those were the words of the prophet who believed that God ruled over history. Those are good words for us today. They are particularly reinforcing for us in moments of testing and trial. The prophet's words dare not be forgotten when we reflect on death and life.

In the early 1800s Charlotte Brontë shared some words of confidence in the midst of trials. Her sister Emily had died. Another sister, Anne, lay dying of tuberculosis. Charlotte wrote to a friend: "I avoid looking forward or backward, and try to keep looking upward . . . the days pass in a slow, dark march; the nights are the worst; the sudden wakings from restless sleep, the revived knowledge that one lies in her grave, and another not at my side, but in a separate and sickbed. However, God is over all."

Words of comfort from friends are precious. The strengthening hand of another who knows about death is helpful. But nothing so supports the soul like the keen consciousness of God's lordship of history. Our times are in His hand. God is over all. He is the One who orders the affairs of history. We are not slugging it out without God's notice.

"Haven't you heard?" asked the prophet. They had heard

a lot, but they hadn't remembered very well. As exiles they had many reasons for questioning God's justice on the earth. Had Israel been more sinful than other nations? Should innocent Israelites suffer along with the guilty? And the longer they doubted God's fairness, the more embittered they grew. They felt more than they thought.

The inequities of this world force us into similar doubts. We fling our "whys" at God, but we should first challenge ourselves—to remember that God controls the world's affairs. The unfairnesses of this life should drive us to the prophet's admonishment: "Lift up your eyes on high and see who has created these stars, the One who leads forth their host by number, He calls them all by name; because of the greatness of His might and the strength of His power not one of them is missing" (Isaiah 40:26, NAS).

The works of God in the universe testify to His lordship. The silent but eloquent heavens reveal God's control of the stormy scenes of history. The earth is tumultuous; the heavens are calm. The rising and falling of kingdoms testify to the lordship of God in history.

My history professor was right. In the midst of the endless dates and events we were to remember in his classes, he left me one healthy notion as I reflect on death and life and suffering: God is the ruling Lord. He rules as Lord of history.

God Is the Restoring Lord

You may be saying about now: So God is in charge: but how long do I have to wait? Is there nothing for me today? Do I have to die before I discover any tangible good in my devotion to this Lord of history? Do I just grieve day after day because of death's intrusion into my life? Is it only pie-in-the-sky-by-and-by that God promises? Isn't there something now?

To such questions the prophet responds affirmatively. One of God's divinest works is to restore strength. One of God's greatest joys is to replenish power where energy has drained away. The prophet says:

> O Jacob, O Israel, how can you say that the Lord doesn't see your troubles and isn't being fair? Don't you yet understand? Don't you know by now that the everlasting God, the Creator of the farthest parts of the earth, never grows faint or weary? No one can fathom the depths of his understanding. He gives power to the tired and worn out, and strength to the weak. Even the youths shall be exhausted, and the young men will all give up. But they that wait upon the Lord shall renew their strength. They shall mount up with wings like eagles; they shall run and not be weary; they shall walk and not faint. Isaiah 40:27-31, LB.

This great God who is Lord of history both sustains and renews. He is a God who is not only transcendent, but immanent. He does not guide at arm's length and from a distance. He is at work among us—restoring us. God isn't simply preoccupied with maintaining the world of nature. His concern is not only to keep the stars from falling out of their orbits. He works here in the world to redeem us—where sin, sickness, and death destroy.

The prophet was not simply exhorting the Israelites to rouse themselves from a spirit of defeatism. That would be whipping a worn-out horse. He proclaims the good news of a resourceful and untiring God. He announces the constant workings of God's boundless energies—workings that only the eyes of faith can adequately behold.

Believers must steel themselves for prolonged efforts and delays. Exasperation and being check-mated becomes part of our experience. But God works. He allows evils to work themselves out. God has the patience to carry out such processes. He outwearies those who oppose Him. His enemies may win many battles, but in the long, long duration of God's war with His and our enemy, He is the Victor.

Gotthold Lessing, German dramatist and critic, said it well in the eighteenth century: "Pursue thy secret path, everlasting Providence; only let me not, because thou art hidden, despair of thee. Let me not despair of thee if thy steps appear to retreat. It is not true that the shortest line is always straight."

People of faith sense God's power of restoration. God provides an exaltation as on wings—when we trust in Him as Lord of history. Henry M. Stanley, the African explorer, once said: "Prayer lifted me hopefully over the 1,600 miles of forest tracks, eager to face the day's perils and fatigues." What kept his head above water? What sustained his spirit in difficult days? The rapture of thinking about God's control and retoration in the world.

Thomas Chalmers once spoke about a year of "mental paradise" when his soul was enraptured with the magnificence of the Godhead. He thought about the ultimate subordination of all things to God's eternal purposes. But at the heart of his thinking was the fact that God was supporting all creation.

The Bible never suggests that God's children will always "fly" ecstatically in the midst of trouble. When the Word assures us of restoration, there is not even a guarantee that we will always "run" in the presence of darkness. Sometimes "walking" is all that God asks. But God says we shall not faint. The Lord declares we will be restored.

The Apostle Peter put it in these words: "And after you have suffered for a little, the God of all grace, who called you to His eternal glory in Christ, will Himself perfect, confirm, strengthen and establish you" (1 Peter 5:10, NAS). One of my young parishioners, still struggling with grief over the loss of her husband, sometimes persuades herself she will never "run" or "fly" again. Even "walking" demands all the spiritual and emotional strength she can generate. But I see the restoration slowly evolving. A more beautiful person emerges as God strengthens and restores her. Many times she remains totally unaware that confirmation and strength are taking place.

But in her life and many others the truth of God's Word becomes reality: after you have suffered awhile, Christ will strengthen and restore you. "Therefore, let those also who suffer according to the will of God entrust their souls to a faithful Creator in doing what is right" (1 Peter 4:19, NAS).

7

Simeon—Reflector on Death and Life

Philip died the day before Christmas. He was an adopted son—the only son of a faithful couple in the church. His death occurred at the age of 35 and after a marriage of only seven years. The painfulness of his death was heightened by its suddenness, unexpectedness, and inexplicable nature. Years had mellowed this young man from a freedom-loving and sometimes rebellious creature to one who loved his wife, respected his parents, and glorified his God.

What do you say to a family celebrating Christmas by burying their only son? In my reflections during those holidays and in preparation for the funeral, another story of parents and a son entered my mind.

A husband and wife brought their son to the Lord's house for dedication. Their hearts rejoiced at the privilege God had granted them in the gift of this firstborn son. Bewilderment swept over them, however, when the pastor-in-residence spoke ominous words about the future of their son.

It was Christmastime but the words they heard were anything but joyous excitement.

A strange mixture of circumstances had led Joseph and
Mary to the temple. Joseph stood as father on this unique
day in his son's life, but really Mary's pregnancy had been
initiated by the Holy Spirit. Yet Joseph proudly called the
child his son. Mary glowed with the thrill and rapture that
can come only from a mother's heart. But on this day she
would hear words that would be troubling and distressing.
They would hear hints of sadness and death.

Aged Simeon uttered those perplexing words to this
happy couple. He lived in the temple. He confidently
believed that he would not die before he had seen the
Messiah. His day arrived. Mary and Joseph brought the
young Jesus to the temple, and Simeon, after blessing the
Child, felt so deeply the fulfillment of his lifelong dream
that he expressed readiness to die. We can learn about death
and life as we reflect on his experience with his three guests.

Happiest Occasions Are Mixed with Sorrow

Simeon, nurtured in the wisdom of God over many years,
recognized that even the happiest occasions are intermin-
gled with sorrow. I suppose only a mother can imagine the
pride with which Mary brought Jesus to the temple that day.
She recognized her unique privilege of being the chosen
mother of the Messiah. For generations mothers had indoc-
trinated their daughters with the possibility they might be
the selected handmaid of God to bring the "chosen one" to
earth. Mary could hardly help but be filled with a sense of
joy and satisfaction.

Simeon's words to Mary almost have a ring of rudeness
and cruelty about them: "Behold, this Child is appointed for
the fall and rise of many in Israel, and for a sign to be op-

posed—and a sword will pierce even your own soul ..."
(Luke 2:34b-35a, NAS). No mother ever heard a more
mixed message—*fall* and *rise*. It was as if Simeon were saying to Mary and Joseph: "In the midst of your joy, just remember that life for you, because of this happy event, will
contain trouble and woe."

We know that the prophecy about trouble ahead wasn't
long in coming. Only a few days passed and they discovered
that a suspicious tyrant named Herod would try to kill their
Son. Joseph and Mary and the Child fled to Egypt to escape
the king's wrath. During the first weeks and months of Jesus'
life the piercing sword already began its troubling work.

The first, thrilling days of motherhood provide a rather
poor and inappropriate time to speak of a new baby's
prospective trials. But if we practiced absolute candor and
honesty, I suppose we would have to say to every new
mother: "Swords and darts and hurts are part of this beautiful package you hold so lovingly in your arms. In the midst
of your joys, prepare for pain." Simeon, wise from the years,
said just that to Mary.

My good friend Gordon MacDonald has shared something of parents' unawareness of future trials when their
children are very young. MacDonald, pastor of Grace
Chapel in Lexington, Massachusetts, writes about his own
naïveté in his most recent book, *The Effective Father*. He
recalls how, when he first looked at the tiny body of his first
son, Mark, he wouldn't have believed that this new life
could actually be a prize over which conflicting forces would
fight. He confesses that for the first two years his protective
instincts allowed for few thoughts of outside interference in
his son's life. Those early years with Mark were so pleasant Mac-
Donald admits that being a father held few fears for him.

But this exuberant father says he was not prepared for the

"blitzkrieg" which soon smashed into their home. The war was targeted right at their son. MacDonald details the lightning-like strikes that neighborhood friends, school, television, and affluence thrust upon that once-innocent son.

I cite this father's observations and experiences only to emphasize that the happiest occasions in life are filled with possibilities for unhappiness. Simeon recognized in Jesus the supreme blessing of the world. But with the blessing, unsurpassed as it was, would come a sword.

In reflecting upon death and life we need to remember that the things in life holding the greatest potential for good also contain an unusual potential for evil. Take atomic power, for instance, one of our greatest discoveries. Yet our generation struggles and fights because we are unable to determine if the hazards in using atomic-produced energy are greater than the good to be derived from it. Or sex—it holds the potential for great good and happiness, but also guilt and heartache.

Simeon recognized that the happiest occasions almost inevitably are mixed with sorrow. My own observation tells me that nothing really worthwhile does not also carry with it possibilities for heartache. Some couples refuse to become parents because the hazards are too great. Fear of unhappiness therefore cancels out forever the possibilities of some of the greatest joys in life. You cannot enjoy the thrills of parenthood without accepting precarious responsibilities. Simeon knew that so well.

I sometimes call on the mother of Philip, the young man who died the day before Christmas. She appears to be a pitiful soul who has lost contact with reality. Perhaps the cares of motherhood hastened the days of being bedfast. And perhaps they did not. But one thing I know. Some of her most rewarding moments in life came because she accepted the risks of motherhood. She welcomed both the hazards and the delights of motherhood.

I doubt that we shall ever escape hazards with anything that holds prospects for good. The astronauts who traveled through space and landed on the moon encountered hazards every moment. Several men died. We reap the benefits of their adventures into space. Somewhere someone pays a price. That's a commentary on life. No good comes without the potential threat of evil. Simeon wisely forewarned Mary and Joseph about the intermingling of happy and sorrowful experiences.

God Redeems in Spite of the Sword

Simeon, truthful as he was with the parents of Jesus, did not play the role of pessimist. He wisely stated that God would work out His plan of redemption in spite of the sword. To be more theologically correct, I probably should say: God would work out His redemption through the sword. Simeon didn't throw in the towel because he knew Joseph and Mary would someday mourn for their Son. Simeon knew God wouldn't be stopped by a Herod who could think only of preserving his own little crumbling kingdom.

The so-called "sword" that pierced the soul of Mary in days to come caused her to weep at the cross. That piercing sword stabbed brutally into her being long after Jesus had died. But redemption came to the world. The cross—the ultimate sword for Mary—was the world's salvation.

When we reflect on death from a biblical standpoint, we must not overlook the fact that He will fulfill His purposes even when we find ourselves stabbed by cruel swords. Sometimes those divine purposes come to fruition in this life; at other times we recognize this earthly life to be a time of preparation and wait for redemption in the next world.

Rufus Jones, Quaker writer and philosopher, has told of going from America to England in 1903. He left his son Lowell in this country, very ill with pneumonia. He thought the son was on the road to recovery. Instead, a relapse occurred, paralysis set in, and the boy died. News of his death reached the father in Liverpool when the ship docked there.

Jones later testified that nothing had ever carried him up into the life of God, or done more to open for him the meaning of love, than the death of his son. He discovered that love could span the separation of father and son. He learned that love can pass beyond the visible and bridge the chasm we sense exists between life and death. The union with his son, he said, knew no end. Eleven years that son had lived and now a sword had pierced his father's heart. But Rufus Jones saw his son's death as God's transplanting of a sacred plant where it could bloom profusely and where it could live more profitably in God's other garden. This man of God, with all the human feelings of an earthly father, recognized that God's redeeming work continues long after the world thinks life is ended.

You never close a chapter in the life of a child of God without opening a new chapter—and a better one. Working His redemption through or in spite of the swords that pierce our souls, God opens us to glory and redemption and power that we cannot fathom.

Simeon knew a secret Mary had not guessed. He glimpsed the death of Jesus on the cross three decades before it happened. He boldly forewarned Mary and Joseph. But the prospect of the piercing sword left Simeon undaunted and unafraid. He saw the salvation that would result. He reflected upon this, and having seen the salvation of the Lord, asked God to take him to heaven. Simeon reflected wisely on death and life. We do well to follow his reflections.

8

Thunder or Angel Voices?

Seminary homiletics classes scarcely qualify as fertile seedbeds for reflecting on death and life. But one sermon delivered in such a setting caught my attention. In the presence of twenty of the most critical listeners any preacher ever had, I listened attentively to a sermon regarding thunder and angels' voices.

I was so impressed by my friend's thoughts that I picked up his ideas and "improved" on his sermon as I faced a small congregation one Sunday morning. As a fledgling preacher, I stumbled and rumbled through the passage I had heard expounded in homiletics class. I was impressed, if no one else was, by my thoughts on "Is It Thunder or Angel Voices You Hear?"

Just sixteen years later the catalyst for that sermon died. He had led a growing congregation in South Dakota and passed away in his thirties, victim of a kidney disease. After a memorial service in the church he served, his body was brought for burial to the town where I pastored. He was a native of this community. Since we had been college and seminary classmates and friends, the young widow requested that I preach the sermon at this second funeral service.

As I sat reflecting on his death, suddenly the recollection of that neophyte sermon rushed into my mind. Thunder or angels' voices? I hastily reached for my concordance to see what precipitated that statement in the New Testament. I found the story:

> "Now my soul has become troubled; and what shall I say, 'Father, save Me from this hour'? But for this purpose I came to this hour. Father, glorify Thy name." There came therefore a voice out of heaven: "I have both glorified it, and will glorify it again." The multitude therefore, who stood by and heard it, were saying that it had thundered; others were saying, "An angel has spoken to Him." John 12:27-29, NAS.

The setting for this incident was the imminent death of Jesus on the cross. Our Lord appeared to be thinking out loud. In the midst of His musings and troubled thoughts, a voice from heaven interrupted both His thoughts and the attention of bystanders. Those within hearing distance arrived at differing conclusions. Some said it thundered. Others sensed they had heard an angel speak.

The experience and reactions of the bystanders at the scene mentioned above provide reflection about death and life. You can chew on that story, savor its taste in your mind, and permit it to nourish your ideas about death.

Similar Experiences Elicit Different Responses

A well-known maxim assures us that "absence makes the heart grow fonder." Experience teaches us that for some persons an additional statement needs to be added: "fonder for someone else." Prolonged separation carries no guarantee that two people who say they love each other will grow in that love in each other's absence. For one, absence does make the heart grow fonder. For others, absence precipitates new friendships that cool former relationships. The same experience can have contrasting effects. When a voice spoke from heaven, some perceived it to be thunder; others concluded an angel had spoken.

A California pastor once shared his personal experience with his people. While he was still a young man, his father died. His brother, feeling keenly the injustice of losing his earthly father, emotionally rejected that death. He never really came to terms with it but simply took a keep-a-stiff-upper-lip approach. Victory in the face of death never became part of his experience as a close bystander of this death. He heard only thunder.

The other son found the courage and strength to accept his father's passing as a part of life. He grieved but he trusted God. He missed the fatherly counsel no longer available, but his life was enriched as he reminisced over the life of a faithful dad. Death proved real and painful, but he heard angels' voices.

For different people the same experience registers different responses. For one, thunder; for another, angel voices.

Jesus rehearsed in the Gospels the story of a homecoming—the story of the prodigal. The one response resembled this: "Praise God! We must celebrate. Kill the fatted calf. Bring a new robe and ring. We must be merry. My son who was dead lives." The father heard angelic news.

Another character in that dramatic story heard little but thunder. He remembered only the waste of financial resources. He rued the fact that the family name had been disgraced. He reminded the father of his own lifelong obedience without any parties honoring him. The younger brother's homecoming created only disturbance for him. He heard the rumbling of ominous thunder. One experience, two responses.

The New Testament tells us about the preaching of John the Baptist. Good news was his message. Repent and be baptized was his plea. Many believed and followed obediently. For them an angel had spoken. But a certain woman, burdened with a guilty conscience, heard only loud thunder when John preached. And when the right moment and opportunity arrived, she asked for John's head on a silver platter—and got it. The same experience had contrary effects.

The first Christmas proved to be a similar experience. To the shepherds and wise men and Simeon and Anna the news of Jesus' birth originated in heaven—angels' voices. But to Herod, suspicious and afraid, pealing of the loudest thunder was all he could hear.

The intensity of the unhappy experience does not necessarily dictate how we respond to misfortune. What some would consider a relatively insignificant trial elicits sounds of thunder. We respond to lesser inconveniences in much the same way as we react to death. Everyday difficulties—high utility bills, a pesky cold, or a dented car fender—are as real to some people as bankruptcy or paralysis is to others. Everyone finds suffering unpleasant. Everyone responds to pain in one of two ways—as troubling thunder or an opportunity to hear one of God's angels speak.

It would be less than honest if we did not say that, strangely enough, we often hear both thunder and angel voices in the same experience. The grieving person moves from one to the other—and often back and forth for a considerable time. We are human. Pain and separation are real. We sense thunder when we must part. Hopefully, however, with God's help and the working of His Spirit, we move from sensing thunder to the realization of angelic messages to our spirits.

Different Responses Depend on the Hearers

The response to an experience depends not so much on the trial as it does on the one being tried. We quickly assume the response issues out from the event. That really isn't true at all. The response depends largely upon us.

People in that crowd with Jesus were conditioned differently and consequently heard differently. Some were tuned to spiritual truths and heard angels. They possessed a sixth sense. There were others who had no way of hearing angels. Their hearts and minds were not fixed on such frequencies. They were people of whom Paul speaks when he describes the natural man who doesn't receive the things of the Spirit of God. So whether or not it was thunder or angel voices depended not on the sound but on the people who heard.

Your preparation of heart determines, to a large extent, what you hear. To appreciate various kinds of music, your ear needs to be conditioned to that kind of music. Dolly Parton and country music holds little appeal for the lover of classical music—and vice versa. If you want to appreciate good literature, preparation is essential. Just so with the so-called tragedies in life—whether we hear thunder or angel voices depends upon how we are prepared to listen. The poet said it in these words:

> Pain built a fence I was quick to hate,
> I clawed at the bars that held me fast;
> But when I learned to be patient at last,
> God took my fence and made it a gate.

When encountered by the child of God who trusts in God's goodness, even death becomes a gate instead of a fence. Thunder and angel voices are both possible responses in the presence of suffering and death.

I recall reading the story of a man who was cruelly crippled in an accident. Part of his face was gone. He was scarcely recognizable. Friends were trying to prepare his wife for the shock she would surely suffer on her first glimpse of her disfigured husband. But when the sad news was shared with her, and the suggestion made that she might be terribly upset, she said "I married a man, not a face."

That experience held the possibilities of thunder or angel voices. She chose to let the sound be angelic. The response depended on her preparation. She listened on the right frequency. She was tuned in to the station where angels speak.

In *A Second Touch*, Keith Miller tells the story of two men traveling in the Southwest brushland at night. The driver lived on a ranch in that area. He was at home in the area, but his passenger claimed the East Coast as home. Suddenly as they approached a cut through a hill, the Easterner saw in the headlights' beams a boulder rolling down into their path ahead. He yelled, clambered into the back seat, and covered his face. The driver, knowing the area well, drove on without a sign of disturbance. He knew that "boulder" was only a tumbleweed.

Both men observed the same object. Both reacted appropriately to what they saw. Yet one turned frantically to despair and fear, while the other's blood pressure scarcely changed. One man lived in a world where tumbleweeds were commonplace. They presented no fear for him. The other saw a giant specter of doom.

Whether we hear thunder or angel voices when death affects us depends on whether or not we have been living on angels' territory. Our response is determined not by the experience so much as by our conditioning. As you and I move along the road of life and around this and that particular bend or curve, our spiritual orientation will determine whether we see boulders or harmless tumbleweeds.

God wants us to hear angel voices in the troubling experiences of life. Most likely we may sense thunder at times. He waits for us to sense the reality of the predicament. He patiently works with us as we move along life's highway with Him.

9

But Even If He
Does Not

The Bible speaks of three men who were too young to die. They succeeded spectacularly in their vocations. They were chosen, under the most unlikely conditions, to take great responsibilities. They climbed the ladder of success by hard work. These three men developed the kind of solid character that was recognized and could be trusted.

Then one day they faced a very difficult decision. Their immediate superior decreed that they bow down and worship him. To refuse meant death. Their refusal might have escaped the notice of the edict-maker, but there were those who watched them closely. Jealous informers of the king observed that they did not obey the mandate. Their disobedience was reported. They were brought before the king who said:

Is it true, Shadrach, Meshach and Abednego, that you do not serve my gods or worship the golden image that I have set up?

Now if you are ready, at the moment you hear the sound of the horn, flute, lyre, trigon, psaltery, and bagpipe, and all kinds of music, to fall down and worship the image that I have made, very well. But if you will not worship, you will immediately be cast into the midst of a furnace of blazing fire; and what god is there who can deliver you out of my hands?" Shadrach, Meschach and Abednego answered and said to the king: "O Nebuchadnezzar, we do not need to give you an answer concerning this. If it be so, our God whom we serve is able to deliver us from the furnace of blazing fire; and He will deliver us out of your hand, O king. *But even if He does not,* let it be known to you, O king, that we are not going to serve your gods or worship the golden image that you have set up." Daniel 3:14-18, NAS, emphasis added.

For three years I watched a young man die. He knew that, barring the direct intervention of God, the cancer working through his body was terminal. One afternoon a small group of us gathered in his home, read the Word together, anointed him with oil, and prayed that God would spare his life. One thing was made very clear before we followed the injunction of James 5, laying hands upon him. The man for whom we had come to pray was insistent that this one thing be very clear: his faith and confidence in God would not be affected regardless of the outcome. He believed God could heal, BUT IF NOT, let it be known to the world that he would serve the living God in confidence so long as he breathed.

I watched him slowly shrivel away until his body was little more than a skeleton covered with skin. Like the Hebrew men of old, he was eager to live. He had a young daughter just beginning school, as well as older children. He supervised a prosperous farming enterprise. He had developed into a leader in his congregation and there seemed to be no human reason why a man in his late forties should be cut off in such a cruel fashion.

This man was willing to declare openly, however, that his confidence in the God he loved did not depend on whether or not he lived. I have often reflected on his attitude and I continue learning as I look at death and life from God's point of view. Shadrach, Meshach, and Abednego can help us reflect on that.

We Accept Less Than the Ideal

Shadrach, Meshach, and Abednego were willing to accept less than the ideal. These three men had it made. By the simple act of bowing down, they would have assured themselves a continuing good position in the empire. Not to bow apparently meant the loss of everything. But when Nebuchadnezzar asked them if the report of their stubbornness was true, they answered: "We really don't even have to answer that question. We know what God can do, and if our God wants to save us, He can. But it doesn't make all that much difference. We just want you to know that we'll serve God if we have to do it by being burned alive."

That's a great attitude. So often I have seen it in the lives of those who faced almost certain death. They loved life but realized they were dying. Sometimes, like the young farmer, they even specifically drew others in to pray with them for healing. But invariably the afflicted, more than the witnesses and participants in the "healing" service, reflect the spirit of the three men facing the blazing furnace. They say in essence, as they face death or life, that they know God can heal. *But even if He does not,* they will not let that erode their trust in a loving all-wise God. They are content to accept less than the ideal.

Isaiah reminds the people of God (Isaiah 40) that those who wait upon the Lord shall renew their strength. Then he explains how that will happen. Some will mount up with wings as eagles. In other words, God's renewing strength can take the form of ecstasy. You can soar in sheer exuberance— and some people have that experience. If one were to conclude, however, that this is God's only way to give strength to His people, then we would be forced to be vastly disappointed when darkness overwhelms us. The person terminally ill with cancer simply cannot always be soaring with ecstasy.

Isaiah leaves room for another eventuality. Another of God's gifts of strength is that "they will run and not get tired" (Isaiah 40:31c, NAS). But once again, this is not the only way we experience God's presence and strength. There are times when there simply is not room nor reason to run and not be weary. There are times when we are tired and weak. We cannot fly; neither can we run.

But Isaiah suggests another alternative. "They will walk and not become weary" (Isaiah 40:31d, NAS). We don't enjoy being slowed to a walk. We aren't accustomed to creeping along inch by inch, just barely maintaining consciousness. We would rather soar or run. But the fact is that sometimes it is sufficient to walk. There are moments, even days and months, perhaps, when trudging along step by step is all we can muster.

The three men facing the heated furnace were willing to take that hazard. I'm confident they preferred life to death. They loved to soar and run as much as you and I do, but they were ready for anything—to walk or even to die. They were willing to accept less than the ideal because even if God did not deliver them, they trusted Him implicitly.

We Recognize Life as a Gift

It may seem impossible for us to walk into our furnaces of fire as confidently as did Shadrach, Meshach, and

Abednego. It is impossible unless we recognize that we don't own our lives. Life is a gift. God has entrusted life to us and we are its stewards.

You cannot walk into the furnace of suffering and face tomorrow confidently unless you also acknowledge that life is a gift. To soar or fly or even walk through the pain and agony of a deteriorating body is impossible unless you can say, "Lord, You can deliver me from this trial by fire, *but if You don't*, I'll keep right on trusting You."

Our most cherished possessions are often gifts. The bamboo plaque that hangs on my study wall is a valued memento of a visit abroad. The beautiful words of one of my spiritual forebears are enjoyed the more because the plaque was a gift. A Philippine believer traveled six hours on two consecutive days to deliver it to me. I treasure that possession. So it is with life. When we recognize that life is a gift, we relish every moment the Giver grants us. The consciousness that life is a gift elicits in us a gratitude that no fiery furnace can destroy.

God's man, Job, learned in so many different ways that his life was a gift. When God spoke to him out of the whirlwind, Job was reminded from where the treasures of the past had come. God reminded him that those evaporated blessings were gifts he did not deserve. That gave Job a sense of perspective about his losses and started him on the upward swing toward healing.

We face life so often as if it belonged to us. If that were true, then to face the heated furnace of trial would, indeed, be catastrophic. Death would be the end. Life would then be confined to earthly existence, and to lose it would mean losing everything. But life does not originate with us, nor can we cling to it as our possession. We are stewards of life. We could relish life more if we acknowledged that it was, every moment, a thing to be savored and enjoyed, even in the midst of pain.

We would care for life more adequately, both physically and spiritually, if we were more conscious of its gift-ness. We would treat life with deeper respect and give ourselves to letting the Giver control it if we realized fully that life is a gift. Fewer people would turn their backs on Christ so nonchalantly if they had conception of the fact that life is a gift and doesn't belong to us. It is far easier to surrender something to the person to whom it belongs in the first place.

The three friends of Daniel perceived that life was a gift. They were no less idealistic than any of us, but if God chose not to deliver them, they would die for Him. They valued their lives no less than any of us do, but they realized something else. They recognized that death, if that became their lot, was simply returning to the Maker what was His all along.

We Can Serve God in Death

Shadrach, Meschach, and Abednego recognized they could serve God by dying as well as by living. I can understand the story of the three men in the furnace only if I believe that conviction permeated their thinking. They believed that God can be served in what looks to us like defeat, as well as in what appears to be victory. "If God delivers us, fine; we'll serve Him gladly. If He doesn't, that's well and good, too, but you can be very sure we won't bow down." These men were not banking all their hopes on being physically delivered. They knew they could serve God dead or alive.

People often make the mistake of thinking that the Bible guarantees they will be rescued from evil and danger. More often then we realize God does deliver from evil. Often we do not consciously recognize that we have been spared by God's merciful hand. But the Bible never guarantees any less earthly disaster for the believer than for the rank unbeliever.

Some of us may be more Hebrew than Christian in our theological orientation to suffering. The people of God, as we read their thoughts in the Psalms and Proverbs, were persuaded that God's spiritual blessings and material prosperity went hand in hand. If a husband and wife lived in godly ways, He would grant them children—and especially male children. Their whole orientation centered around the belief that tangible good followed *being* good. I am willing to grant that God, knowing how far along His Hebrew children were in their spiritual pilgrimmage, often operated according to that view. But God was also trying to get them to move from that position. He was pushing toward the New Testament view that no child of God can evaluate his goodness based on the abundance of material blessings.

Many people still operate on Old Testament principles. We can't fathom why God should allow suffering for people who live in His ways. Somehow we forget that God said the rain falls both on the just and the unjust. No biblical guarantees assure us that we will be rescued from all physical evil and dangers. The Bible is explicit in saying that whether or not we are physically rescued isn't the crux of the matter. We serve God in either event.

The Book of Hebrews recites a lengthy list of heroes who were miraculously delivered. We thrill to the stories of Abel, Enoch, Noah, Abraham, Sarah, and a host of others mentioned in Hebrews 13. By faith they endured and were delivered.

But have you pondered the rest of the chapter? After rehearsing the heroics of lesser-known saints like Gideon,

Barak, Jephthah—who conquered kingdoms and a variety of enemies—we read that "others were tortured ... others experienced mockings and scourgings, yes, also chains and imprisonment. They were stoned, they were sawn in two, they were tempted, they were put to death with the sword.... And all these, having gained approval through their faith, did not receive what was promised, because God had provided something better" (Hebrews 11:35-37, 39, NAS).

Those were men and women of faith, but they were not delivered. Nevertheless, their commendation from God rates equally as high as that of the supernaturally preserved. Like the three men facing the furnace and the king's wrath, the unrescued were saying, "If God delivers us, and we know He can, fine; we'll continue living and serving. But if not, we'll still serve Him. We can serve God in death as well as in life."

Recently I stood at the bedside of a child of God whose body was ravaged by the onslaughts of disease. She realized that her life on this earth was short, unless God intervened. She loved life. She had dear ones for whom she would have loved to live. But as she prayed she said to God, "I would be happy to serve you in life, but if that is impossible, I shall be happy to serve you in death." Not many weeks later she made her exit from this life into the life that never ends. She was willing to accept less than the ideal. She saw her physical existence, as well as her spiritual life, as a gift from God and was prepared to turn her body and spirit over to Him. She recognized the possibility of serving her Master in death as well as in life. She faced the furnace like the friends of Daniel. "If it be so, our God whom we serve is able to deliver us.... *But even if he does not* ... we are not going to serve your gods" (Daniel 3:17-18, NAS, emphasis added).

10

Preferring the Gift Over the Giver

Three of us sat around a swimming pool across the street from the medical center where 30-year-old Dennis, the lone survivor of a fiery airplane crash, had spent four weeks in the burn unit. We discussed God's will for Dennis. His soon-to-be-widow realized her prayerful dream of healing was not taking place. We all knew that, humanly speaking, this father of two young sons would not live.

Yet we discussed the possibility of healing, for some good friends were firmly convinced God should and would heal Dennis. Dennis's wife wondered out loud if the Lord did not want to bring a kind of healing other than the restoration of a human body. Perhaps God wanted to heal her, her sons, and others, rather than the hopelessly burned body of Dennis.

Her observation reminded me of a comment made only a few hours earlier by an Australian layman. He spoke of a good friend who had been involved in the charismatic movement. Their association was severed when his friend came to care more for the gifts than the giver.

Whenever we face separation through death and ask for the gift of healing, we need to be clear about the relationship of the gifts to the Giver. The story of Jesus at the well at Sychar and the Samaritan woman provides insight into this relationship. When Jesus came to the well, He asked a surprised Samaritan woman for a drink. Then He said:

> If you knew the gift of God, and who it is who says to you, "Give Me a drink," you would have asked Him, and He would have given you living water. She said to Him, "Sir, You have nothing to draw with and the well is deep; where then do You get that living water? You are not greater than our father Jacob, are You, who gave us the well, and drank of it himself, and his sons, and his cattle?" Jesus answered and said to her, "Everyone who drinks of this water shall thirst again; but whoever drinks of the water that I shall give him shall never thirst; but the water that I shall give him shall become in him a well of water springing up to eternal life." John 4:10-14, NAS.

We Prefer the Gift

Jesus recognizes that as we face issues of life and death we are prone to prefer the gift over the Giver. Though the Samaritan woman reached for the gift of water, Jesus made no attempt to embarrass her. He reasoned with her but did not scold. She was a human being who tired of coming to the well daily for water. To hope for water that would satisfy her thirst forever was a natural wish. Jesus recognized that.

He understands that in us also. He does not scold us when we find ourselves pleading for the gift of healing more than we desire the Giver. He doesn't wince if and when we weep because the gift—the life of a loved one—has been taken from us. He wept, too.

He knows how human it is to desire the gift of life for a

loved one. He is not unhappy with us because we pray for
the healing of one who is painfully and tragically ill in body
and mind. He treated the woman at the well kindly, although she didn't know what was best for her. Our Lord will
do no less for us. He knows how we feel. He knows we often
prefer the gift over the Giver.

That preference was first seen in the Garden of Eden.
Adam and Eve soon yearned for one gift that was not
intended to be theirs. They had everything else, but the fruit
of that one tree looked so desirable. They chose, like we
often do, the fruit rather than obedience to the Giver.

When the people of Israel journeyed in the wilderness,
God gave them gifts—manna and quail and fire and clouds.
But it didn't take long until the people could think only of
the tangible gifts. They forgot that these things were only
symbolic of God's presence and care for them. The gifts
were to remind them of the Giver, but they preferred the
gifts to the Giver.

In Jesus' day people had the same attitude. He performed
miracles and provided free food for them. But the people
preferred the healing and food over the Giver. Thus Jesus
said sadly one day: "You seek Me . . . because you ate of the
loaves, and were filled" (John 6:26, NAS). On another occasion He said, in effect, "Your only interest in me is that you
think I might be a judge and divider, redistributing material
things, and giving you a bigger share in them."

God is not opposed to distributing gifts for us to enjoy.
The New Testament reiterates that as a good Father one of
His pleasures is to distribute good things to His children. He
is not surprised nor particularly hurt because we want the
gift. He does not upbraid us for praying that a young husband and father with a brilliant future ahead of him, who is
suddenly reduced to a near vegetable, should be mi-

raculously healed. He doesn't stand in condemnation as we suffer and miss the presence of someone we have learned to love. He does not become harsh with us. He knows our proneness to prefer the gift over the Giver.

The Giver Is Better Than the Gift

Jesus wants us to recognize that the Giver is better than the gift. He said, in effect, to the Samaritan woman: "You are looking for water. If you really understood who I am, you would ask me and I would satisfy your deepest needs. If you knew the truth, you would ask for the Giver and then the gift of liquid water—which only slakes the thirst for a moment—would come to take on lesser significance. Everybody who drinks of this water (me) shall never thirst again. His deepest needs shall be met." Jesus was gently, but firmly, showing the woman that the possession of the Giver was better than the possession of the gifts.

The young woman whose husband was dying was right. In this instance, at least, in God's permissive will, an accident had occurred and God, in essence, had said, "While I love to give gifts, even healing of the body, I will come to you with healing you have not begun to understand. Believe that my presence as the Great Giver is better than the gift of life itself." When God says that, He does so, knowing how much we hurt. But He is saying to us as He did to the woman at the well, "Just trust me, the Giver, and I will create in you a well of water that will simply never run dry. Believe me when I tell you that it is better to have the Giver than to possess the gift."

In every human heart there is a thirst for something that only Jesus Christ can satisfy. Sinclair Lewis once wrote about a businessman who repudiated moral standards and behaved badly. The woman whom he loved listened to him and then said, "On the surface we seem quite different, but deep down we are fundamentally the same. We are both desperately unhappy about something—and we don't know what it is."

That's precisely why Jesus longs to have us learn that Jesus Christ himself is to be preferred over His gifts. He knows what we need most desperately. He knew how badly this woman needed running water in her house, but He knew something more. He knew that her greatest need was the giver of the living water, not the ordinary water. He could give her that water only if she would receive it. He can give the presence of the Giver today to anyone who will receive him by repentance and trust.

The beautiful thing about preferring Christ to His gifts is that as we receive Him we receive many wonderful gifts. The Apostle Paul once urged some Corinthians to contribute to a fund for the poor. They felt he was asking too much; he was trying to make them poor. But Paul said:

> And God is able to make all grace abound to you, that always having all sufficiency in everything, you may have an abundance for every good deed; as it is written, "He scattered abroad, He gave to the poor, His righteousness abides forever." Now He who supplies seed to the sower and bread for food, will supply and multiply your seed for sowing and increase the harvest of your righteousness. 2 Corinthians 9:8-10, NAS.

We pray for the gift and sometimes God does not see fit to grant it. We pray for healing of a sick body; and death, rather than life, is the answer. God chooses not to grant the gift in the form for which we have prayed. But He wants to grant us the Giver—and He will. He will pour out his mercies on the widows and the orphans, as the psalmist says in his description of the loving God, "a father of the fatherless and a judge for the widows" (Psalm 68:5a, NAS).

God never wants us to be ungrateful for His gifts. So today He tells us to be grateful for bodies that are strong and well—and for a thousand other gifts—but He says lovingly, "Let your chief desire be the possession of the Giver. When you have Him, then even when the gifts are withdrawn, you still have the best—the Giver. His presence cannot be taken from you."

11

Loosening the Ropes of Our Tent

In the Apostle Paul's culture, every Roman meal ended with a sacrifice. A cup of wine was taken in hand and poured out to the gods. When the Apostle Paul wrote to his trusted, young friend, Timothy, he apparently recalled that Roman custom. He used the word for "pouring out" to describe his oncoming death:

> For I am already being poured out as a drink offering, and the time of my departure has come. I have fought the good fight, I have finished the course, I have kept the faith; in the future there is laid up for me the crown of righteousness, which the Lord, the righteous Judge, will award to me on that day; and not only to me, but also to all who have loved His appearing. 2 Timothy 4:6-8, NAS.

The greatest missionary of ancient times was saying, "The day is ended; it is time to rise and go; and my life is to be poured out to God."

What would you say to your closest friends if you knew

your earthly life would be concluded within days or even hours? The Apostle Paul possessed no premonition that he would die by illness or accident. Rather, he recognized that within hours the executioner's knife would sever his head from his body.

The apostle had some advice for his friends. In the verse preceding the passage quoted above, he said, in effect, "Stand ready . . . don't be afraid . . . leave nothing undone that ought to be done." And then he followed with reasons why he was confident in giving such instructions: "I'm sharing this with you because I won't be around much longer. My time has expired. I will be on my way to heaven soon."

God's servant, Paul, was so satisfied with his life that he was content to die. That satisfaction provided the motivation for willingly loosening himself from this earthly life. As I reflect on that readiness to be relieved of earthly life, I sense this man perceived some things about death and life that can profit all who live and ultimately die.

Struggling Between Good and Evil

The apostle was under no illusion that life was comfortable. He recognized that, for one living under the leadership of Christ, it had to be assumed there would be a struggle between good and evil.

Paul indicates that "the time of my departure has come" (2 Timothy 4:6b, NAS). The word for "departure" is a very vivid one in the Greek language. Its meaning describes effectively how the apostle looked upon life and the prospect of departing from it. The original word for "departure" connotes something with which any ancient farmer would be familiar. It is the word for unyoking an animal from the shafts of a plow. The word is also used for loosening bonds or chains. It is the word for loosening the ropes of a tent. It is the word used to describe loosening the mooring ropes of a ship at anchor.

From the original meanings of the word used by the writer, we can readily draw conclusions about how Paul saw life and death. Death was rest from toil and struggle. Death was liberation and release. Death was picking up camp, setting off on another journey. Death was pulling up anchor and sailing for a final destination.

Inherent in each of the word-pictures suggested by "departure" is the admission that struggle lies at the heart of every Christian life. The Bible honestly portrays life as no bed of tulips. It never camouflages the fact that the garden of life has its thorns and thistles. The Scriptures never gloss over the uncomfortable and painful. God's Word calls life a battle—a struggle between good and evil.

As Paul rehearses his life and faces the prospect of dying, his conclusions harmonize with the biblical view. He simply remarks that he has fought long and hard. He is not sentimental about life. He does not suggest that our earthly existence consists of a series of joyful, pleasant experiences heaped together in one giant, glorious package. Life involves fighting.

My reflections about life and death have been influenced considerably by watching people die, some very quickly and others painfully and slowly. I recall the anxiousness of sitting in a hospital intensive-care room while physicians treated one of my closest friends after a cardiac arrest. He was only 46 years old, and the last half day of his life epitomized struggle at its worst. More than once his heart stopped beating. But each time the physician's massage of the heart or a quickly administered surge of electrical current reactivated the struggling vital organ. But then I watched sadly as the trailing lines of the electrocardiograph tapered off into a flat line, and I knew that the struggle had ended.

That young husband and father knew about another struggle—between good and evil. He knew the times when his natural inclinations led him in ways that were not God's. He remembered, not with pleasure, the struggles of youth and the pressures that surround the young. Those struggles no doubt motivated him to serve as a youth sponsor in our congregation for many years. He experienced firsthand, both in life and death, the reality of the struggle between good and evil.

The Old Testament people of God, warned by Jehovah of the struggle in the world, heard Him say: "I have set before you life and death, blessing and curse; therefore choose life, that you and your descendants may live, loving the Lord your God, obeying his voice, and cleaving to him; for that means life to you and length of days" (Deuteronomy 30:19, RSV).

God does not gloss over the struggle. He is not unaware nor unfeeling about the battle being staged in the world between good and evil. But He asks us to choose in the face of that conflict. He allows freedom so that men and women can go His way or another. But the consequences of the choice are clearly outlined. Loving your God produces life in its purest sense; refusing Him results in death and evil.

When we reflect on God's view of death and life, we cannot afford to lose sight of the scriptural truth that struggle is one of the characteristics of the believer's death. The Christian constantly is forced to choose sides. He lives in an arena of warfare.

And when death knocks at life's door, it is like loosening the ropes of a tent. The knots of the rope are settled around the stakes, firm and unyielding, but departing from this life no doubt frees us, as the ropes free the tent from the ground.

A tearing asunder is part of that death process. Struggle lies at the heart of that separation.

Willingness to Do God's Work

The Apostle Paul was content, even eager, to do his part of God's work. He spoke of finishing his course. I'm fascinated that Paul never said anything about getting all his work done. I'm confident his conception of God's work in the world precluded any thought of ever finishing all the work he might be able to do.

More work always remained. Wider horizons constantly appeared before the apostle's eyes. He never finished the work; he only finished the course—his portion of the task—assigned to him.

When we reflect on the biblical view of death and life, we do well to remember that we are not compelled or even asked to do all of God's work. The 46-year-old implement dealer I mentioned earlier left a lot of unfinished work when he passed so swiftly off the scene. Humanly speaking, many opportunities lay ahead for a man with his experience.

Fortunately, God never asks any of us to get all of the work done. He simply asks that we be faithful for our share of the work. I'm persuaded there is a sense in which all of us should leave unfinished work when we die. God has apportioned a small part of His ministry in the world to us. We are responsible for our "slice" of the pie, but the pie (God's plan for the world) surpasses any perception we will ever have of it. God asks only that we faithfully perform our portion of the work.

I know from personal experience that all the work never gets done. People knock at my door and the telephone rings after I am asleep and before I awake. Longer working days do not resolve the problem of unfinished work. Nothing grieves nor haunts me more than the realization of work that remains undone. Somehow I am prone to think I should accomplish everything there is to do.

A proper reflection upon God's design for our lives demands a consciousness that we will never get all His work done. God never asks that of anyone. He wants us willingly and eagerly to seize the opportunities to do His work, but God determines our portion of the work. Then He lifts our anchor, loosens our burden, and pulls up the stakes. And we are relieved.

I'm confident that in Paul's mind there were a hundred blueprints for work that needed to be done for God. But God never planned for him to construct everything about which he had dreamed. Paul recognized that and thus was able to conclude: "And now the time has come for me to stop fighting—and rest." He was facing squarely the fact that he wouldn't be around much longer. His time had run out. He would soon be ushered into the splendors of heaven. He hadn't finished all the work he had envisioned. But he was content. He had done what he could. He had finished his course. He was satisfied to move along.

When viewed from that perspective, even death at a comparatively young age is not a tragedy. To die in the prime of one's productive years, then, is not cruel and inhumane. God expects faithfulness from His people. He entrusts only a portion of His work to us. Then He loosens the ropes of this earthly house, this tent, our body, and bids us move on.

Trusting God to Finish the Work

When the Apostle Paul bade farewell to his friends, he left them more than an encouragement to continue doing their work for God. He expressed confidence that the Father would bring everything unfinished to completion. He didn't hesitate to urge his fellow believers to continue bringing others to Christ and leave nothing undone that ought to be done. But he didn't stop with those words. He confidently voiced the persuasion that there was a crown waiting for him, which the Lord, the righteous Judge, would give him.

On another occasion the apostle wrote: "I know who it is in whom I have trusted, and am confident of his power to keep safe what he has put into my charge, until the great Day" (2 Timothy 1:12, NEB). He expressed confidence that God would finish the total plan for the ages.

The belief that a project or enterprise will be finalized, regardless of one's own future involvement, is a comfort and strength to anyone forced to withdraw from such an endeavor. To be assured that a work of love will be culminated, even in our absence, brings cheer and encouragement.

Sometime ago a comparatively young man died in a fiery airplane crash. For years the community had nurtured the hope that someone would establish a respectable restaurant in our town. That dream was in the process of being realized when the crash occurred. The redecoration of an existing building and the rough structure for an attractive addition stood halfway finished the day the fatal accident occurred. And who was the heart and soul and financier behind the construction of this much-needed eating establishment? The dead pilot.

All work ceased immediately. Throughout the community people pondered the future of this disrupted dream. But the indefiniteness lasted only a single day. In the midst of intense grief, the young widow ordered the contractor to return to work on the building two days after the crash. She was deeply persuaded that her husband would want it that way. He would want the project to come to fruition.

Confidence that God will bring His work to completion buoys the hope of one struggling with the prospect of his own demise. Knowing that the living Lord never allows His kingdom work to stand nakedly half-completed gives confidence to let loose of life and breath. Trusting that God will finish not only His work but our personal perfection (sanctification) frees us to turn loose of the ropes of this earthly tent—our vulnerable bodies.

A part of the apostle's last will and testament was the assurance that his Master's "construction job" in the world did not depend only upon Paul. The one who called himself the "least of the apostles" had played his role. That was all God asked.

Before his death the devout Quaker, George Fox, addressed a letter to his friends. He sealed it and wrote on the outside: "not to be opened before the time." In 1691, a year after his death, the letter was found. Upon opening this carefully prepared treatise, his friends found a message of hope and light. There was an outline of what Fox believed. His legacy to his followers was not houses and barns, not costly cathedrals and power, but a quiet faith and life-giving confidence in the future with God.

We, too, can find the confidence to give assent to the "loosening of the ropes of our tent." That confidence comes from recognizing we struggle with evil. Release is possible when we feel good about having borne our portion of the Lord's work, not someone else's. Death can come with greater grace when we trust God to complete the good work that lies unfinished.

12

He Made Me a Polished Arrow

A colleague in the ministry and I sat in my study stunned. We had just received news of the death of still another colleague. In a seemingly avoidable accident in British Columbia a servant of God was snatched from us. He was a husband and father to his family. For me he was a confidante in times of struggle and decision-making. For many he was an instructor in Bible in a college. For others he was an administrator. Now he was gone—suddenly and cruelly erased from the earthly scene. A drunken driver's inability to maneuver his vehicle down the highway had resulted in death for God's servant.

Thoughtfully and prayerfully, anticipating the arrangements the family and we would have to make for the memorial service, we reflected once more on death and life. Why does God allow the ungodly to be the instruments of destruction for the children of God? Where is God when a 48-year-old servant, in the prime years of his life, with one quick swoop is ushered out of our presence? We needed him.

In the midst of my reflections, my attention was focused on the words of Isaiah to a despondent people of God. For purposes of instruction and comfort the prophet had exclaimed:

> Listen to me, O coastlands, and hearken, you peoples from afar. The Lord called me from the womb, from the body of my mother he named my name. He made my mouth like a sharp sword, in the shadow of his hand he hid me; he made me a polished arrow, in his quiver he hid me away. And he said to me, "You are my servant, Israel, in whom I will be glorified." But I said, "I have labored in vain, I have spent my strength for nothing and vanity; yet surely my right is with the Lord, and my recompense with the Lord my God." Isaiah 49:1-4, RSV.

Isaiah served as God's voice to Israel. The people of God became despondent. The work did not exhaust them; it was the feeling that nothing resulted from their labors.

To sense the loss of a loved one snatched by death from your side produces exhaustion. The senselessness of life consumes the soul if it is not adequately armed with the mind of God. We may well feel in our darkest moments what Gregory of Nazienzen wrote to a friend in the fourth century: "All that is honorable is perishing; evils are naked; our voyage is in the dark; there is a beacon nowhere; Christ is sleeping."

The words of Isaiah encouraged me as I reflected on what he said about death and life. To those of us who tend to believe the church and kingdom are forever collapsing, his words engender life and hope. We are all servants. His words were spoken to servants and thus apply to all of us.

The Lord Calls Servants

The consciousness of being called can be a tremendous

bulwark of support in difficult moments. When I was a young man, my congregation "elected" me into the ministry. It was a passing custom in our denomination to choose preachers from the pew. Having sensed the call of God in my life, but never expressing that urgency to anyone, God's people said: "We believe God is calling you; we confirm that call." That has often strengthened me. Repeatedly I have returned in my mind to that day thirty years ago when someone reinforced what I felt was the call of God.

When we reflect on the seemingly strange ways of God in death and life, it is helpful to see ourselves as God's called ones. Isaiah spoke of being called from the womb. His testimony is that he was called from his birth. Even in the body of his mother God remembered him—"he named my name" (Isaiah 49:1b, RSV).

The prophet had come to an unshakable conviction that his servanthood originated with God. That ownership by God sustained his faith and lifted his beleaguered spirit. He had been in God's mind long before he had begun to serve Him.

The calling of God was a repeated theme in Isaiah's message. "Fear not, for I have redeemed you; I have called you by name, you are mine" (Isaiah 43:1b, RSV). "Every one who is called by my name, whom I created for my glory, whom I formed and made" (Isaiah 43:7, RSV) is the description of each of the children of God. And again the prophet has the Lord saying of His witnesses, "And my servant whom I have chosen" (Isaiah 43:10b, RSV).

The sense of God's ownership through His call relaxed my troubled spirit as I pondered the death of my colleague. If God chose him before he was born to be His servant, should I quarrel about the time of his release from this life? If his preaching and teaching evolved from a call of God that was in effect before he saw his first daylight, could I argue with the Lord about his all-too-soon departure?

The sense of God's mark of ownership upon His children can eradicate much of the confusion and anger that overwhelms us when death walks into our experiences. The rebellion lurking in my heart about my friend's sudden demise dissipated as I lingered thoughtfully about God's call on his life. If only we had done the calling, we might legitimately question the shortness of his service. But God called. He had called and He could also call home.

A pastor once met one of his students and said, "You are really a gifted young man." The student blushed immediately, as if the pastor had praised him. Sensing the student's embarrassment and his misunderstanding of what had been said, the pastor followed by saying, "You don't need to blush, for I did not say that you are a splendid personality or a wonderful fellow. I merely said that gifts have been bestowed upon you for which you are responsible to Another who gave them to you."

That is true of every servant whom God has called. The calling of God implies that our capacities are gifts from Him. And if we are stewards of gifts, we may well leave the time span of the gifts' usefulness to the Giver.

Helmut Thielicke, the German pastor who lived through the hellish days of World War II in Berlin, has spoken about what he learned in those dark days. He recognized he was a called and chosen servant. That recognition came only when the bombs began to fall. Previously he had become accustomed to looking at the books in his study and saying, "All this is my scholarship and wisdom. It belongs to me. It is my extended self." But when the houses collapsed and the churches burned, he began to think differently. He saw that all his gifts were indeed gifts. God owned them because God had chosen Helmut Thielicke to be His servant. We do well to ponder God's ownership when reflecting on death. We were in God's mind before we were born. We belong to Him. We have been called. That takes a heavy burden from us—we do not have to decide when the use of those gifts shall be terminated on this earth.

The Lord Molds Servants

God never gets caught unawares. He never calls a man but what He equips and fashions him as well. Isaiah said, "He made my mouth like a sharp sword . . . he made me a polished arrow, in his quiver he hid me away" (Isaiah 49:2, RSV).

Once again I allowed my wounded spirit to contemplate how God had effectively used my colleague while he was alive. The Lord had smoothed and polished that human shaft so that it pierced the hearts and lives of young and old alike.

We are not only called servants—and therefore valuable to God. We become prepared servants, sharpened as tools for His service. He wants instruments with keen cutting edges. He wills for us to become adept and skilled. God had done that with my teacher friend whose life was snuffed out so quickly.

But what struck me with increased forcefulness as I reflected upon Isaiah's words was the little expression "in his quiver he hid me away" (Isaiah 49:2c, RSV). That's a beautiful picture of God's servant. He is called and chosen. The Lord molds him, sharpens him, and makes him a useful and effective tool. But the arrow is to be used at the discretion of God. The polished shaft can be placed in the bow and thrust through the air to do its work. But the prepared weapon can also be hidden in the Lord's quiver. The servant does not determine when and where he will be thrust into God's work. He does not always know in which direction he will be sent. He may well be kept in God's quiver for use at the appropriate, God-appointed time.

The servant of God, chosen and molded, is like a shaft or arrow possessed by God. He stands ready at God's beck and call. He is subject to God's appointments. If that is true, then I must relax when one of God's polished shafts is withdrawn from what I see as useful service. I cannot object when death ends a career that seems all too short. The Lord in His wisdom not only calls and molds his arrows; he decides whether or not they are shot into the mainstream of daily life and when they are replaced into the quiver. Who am I to struggle against His lordship?

The Lord Uses and Rewards Servants

God never chooses servants without equipping them; He never equips them without somehow using them in His kingdom. The people of God in Isaiah's day thought they had labored in vain. They saw no fruits. They envisioned themselves to be a prepared people with no work nor any reward. And the prophet apparently was prone to join them in that song of lament. He confessed that he felt he had spent his strength for nothing.

The prophet, however, was not without confidence in God's use of His servants. "Yet surely my right is with the Lord, and my recompense with my God" (Isaiah 49:4b, RSV). The proper perspective on death and life demands that we recognize both the Lord's use of our polished shafts and His reward for that service. When God calls and molds and uses, He will also reward.

Sometimes that reward appears to be delayed. My teacher friend did not have the joy of seeing the harvest of much of his instruction. When he watched the apparent listlessness of some of his students, he must have hoped that the slumbering seeds he had planted would one day germinate and grow. And so it has been. There are effective shafts and arrows, polished for service, in the Lord's field today because this man labored even for such a short time.

The reward comes. Sometimes it seems quite delayed, but it comes. God never wastes anything. He uses those polished arrows and they strike their mark. We may remain completely unaware of their effectiveness, but God never forgets. He will reward.

There are times when God rewards by transferring His servant to a greater work. Borden of Yale died on the mission field at the age of 25. Dr. Robert Speer wrote to Borden's grieving mother: "God has more important work to be done elsewhere than it is possible for men to do here on earth . . . he needed your son in the ministry of those who serve him day and night."

As I continued to ponder Isaiah's words and my friend's death, I began to see him rewarded. He had been promoted to a greater service. And even then his work as a polished shaft would not cease. He was a graduate with highest honors, but the effects of his life would continue to bear fruit.

Just yesterday a friend shared with me one of the strange ways in which God works. Her sister, victim of one unhappy marriage and unsatisfied with a second, had prayed for a renewed heart for her husband. She had gone so far as to pray that God could do anything He wished to bring that awakening into reality. In an automobile accident that left two daughters unharmed, the woman was killed. The polished arrow was returned to the quiver. She was another graduate with honors. But the story has not ended. Within a

week of her death her widowered husband and another
person have committed their lives to Christ.

I do not accept the theory that God deliberately took one
life so that two others could discover new life. But I do
believe God uses molded, called, useful, and polished arrows
to bring about His will. God does reward. Sometimes death
itself is that reward. As I reflect upon death and life, I listen
not only to Isaiah's words but to those of the poet:

> They pass from work to greater work
>   Who rest before their noon;
> Oh, God is very good to them,
>   They do not die too soon.

13

Throw Your Bread on the Water

You learn to live by dying, the Bible says. But you also discover how to die admirably by learning to live biblically. Death and life interwine to such an extent that one affects the other appreciably. That is why, when we reflect upon death or life, we cannot separate them. In no way am I simply suggesting that the manner of our earthly life determines the destination of our spirit at death.

I have observed that people, in their older years, usually demonstrate, with increased intensity, those characteristics learned and practiced while younger. The dour, pessimistic, complaining person seldom reverses his attitudes and behavior when advancing age afflicts the body and spirit. Similarly, the contented, cheerful, optimistic person often retains that positive spirit as he grows older.

If you want to die with dignity, the best insurance is to live with dignity. What you have practiced in active life determines how you respond to the prospect of death.

I once watched for months as one of my parishioners wasted away, having suffered a stroke, but he lived for several years after he was incapacitated. Hospital attendants observed that in his weakest moments he never refused to eat. Some surmised this was the result of knowing firsthand the intense pangs of hunger. He had seen men and women die for lack of food. He had personally envisioned death for want of bread.

When this man died, I reflected upon his life. I thought of a passage of Scripture that served as the basis for the memorial service meditation.

> Cast your bread on the surface of the waters, for you will find it after many days. Divide your portion to seven, or even to eight, for you do not know what misfortune may occur on the earth. If the clouds are full, they pour out rain upon the earth; and whether a tree falls toward the south or toward the north, wherever the tree falls, there it lies. He who watches the wind will not sow and he who looks at the clouds will not reap. Ecclesiastes 11:1-4, NAS.

Interpretations abound about the meaning of this passage. Some insist this is a reference to merchants sending their goods on ships abroad, hopefully making a profit. Others contend this is a reference to an Egyptian practice of broadcasting rice on the mud and water of the swollen Nile, hoping the seed would sprout and grow. Still others have concluded the writer suggested: "Be generous, do not be narrow in your liberality; scatter the seeds of kindness on the thankless and unpredictable waters. Be certain that sooner or later you will be rewarded."

I have no settled opinion about the correctness of any of those views. I do believe that those words contain untapped reservoirs of ideas for reflection upon death and life. My interpretation will be influenced by the life and death of the

man who knew from personal experience the gnawing pains
of hunger. He never forgot. That memory influenced the
manner in which he lived and died.

Admission of Goodness Being Wasted

Doing good subjects one to the danger of losing. The
bread cast upon the water stands a chance of being lost. The
wisdom writer suggested that you divide your "portion to
seven, or even to eight, for you know not what evil may happen on earth" (Ecclesiastes 11:2 RSV). The intimation is that
there are hazards to distributing your bread on the waters.
That would be true in shipping commodities by boat, sow-
ing rice along the Nile, or scattering seeds of kindness.

Living under the lordship of Christ includes the aware-
ness that goodness may be wasted. Christlike living implies
the recognition that we may never behold the positive
results of bread spread on the waters. We must be prepared
for disappointment. We sow the deeds of mercy in faith,
from conviction and principle, not from an assurance of visible and immediate success.

The man to whom I referred earlier in the chapter
responded to his own experience of hunger when young by
devoting himself to a ministry to hungry people around the
world. Working with Mennonite Central Committee and its
concern for the unfortunate consumed much of his energies.
CARE packages by the hundreds were sent through his
initiative to needy people abroad. He spoke forcefully at
conventions and in congregations urging his peers to
minister to the needs of the hungry.

That man was exposed to considerable criticism. People
insisted that contributed food and money were wasted. Men
and women refused to join his crusade for casting bread on
the waters because the wrong people would be the re-

cipients. They were sometimes correct, no doubt. But that did not dismay nor discourage the efforts of our brother. He did not obey God because His goodness would all find its rightful place. He obeyed in casting bread on the waters because it was the godly thing to do. He was the broadcaster; God would supervise and care for the harvest.

You should be prepared to lose when you practice goodness in the name of Christ. No guarantee of success has been assured. You cast your bread upon the waters, knowing that some of it will sink beneath the sea. But you cast it, nevertheless, because it is right. Living in that fashion constitutes part of what it means to prepare to die peacefully, contentedly, and with a good conscience.

A Warning Against Excess Caution

The wisdom writer in Ecclesiastes suggests that "he who observes the wind will not sow; and he who regards the clouds will not reap" (Ecclesiastes 11:4, RSV). Good business economics would suggest that the farmer should not sow indiscriminately. The Word of God implies there is a place for letting the seed fall far and wide. The picture in the verse is that of a farmer carefully watching the weather to find the proper moment to plant. In the contemporary scene, it would suggest studying the weather patterns, observing the high and low pressure movements, and scanning the radar reports before going to the field to sow.

The inference of the biblical writer is that such a man never reaps a harvest. His cautiousness precludes ever garnering in a crop. Similarly, if you wait to invest deeds of kindness in the lives of people until all the circumstances are favorable, you will rarely cast your bread on the waters. The farmer can delay his plans at every sign of changing weather. The Christian believer can hesitate at every sign of uncertainty—searching for the most productive time to plant—and he will likely never harvest a crop of goodness.

Lack of knowledge about the effectiveness of our deeds should not lead us to inaction. We must not be guilty of saying: "I'm wary of changes that may arise; my labors may prove to be unprofitable; my devotion may not be appreciated; the recipients of my actions may be unresponsive or ungrateful. Therefore I shall not do good."

We ought rather to say: "I do not know what is coming. I have no assurance of reward. I know little about my span of time here on earth or the opportunities granted to me. But I must lose no time and waste no strength. I must involve myself in the needs of people. I cannot tell which words will fall like water on rocks, or which deeds like seeds on fertile soil. Therefore my best is the least I can do."

Jesus goaded His disciples into pouring out their lives for Him and the gospel's sake. His was not a cautious spirit nor is ours to be one of timidity. He cast bread upon the waters and some of His deeds were stomped into the mud. We may share that indignity.

The Turks have an old saying: "Do good, throw it into the water; if the fish does not know it, God does." The biblical view of the stewardship of life resembles that. Excess caution is not characteristic of the faithful disciple of Christ. Goethe expressed a similar thought in these words:

> Was willst du untersuchen,
>   Wohin die Milde fliest!
> Ins Wasser wirf deine Kuchen;
>   Wer weiss wer sie geniesst?

> Wouldst thou too narrowly inquire
>   Whither thy kindness goes!
> Thy cake upon the water cast;
>   Whom it may feed who knows?

Living so that death is not an unwelcome intruder demands thrusting yourself into God's work of ministering to people. Excess caution is foreign to that strategy.

A Promise of Eventual Reward

When the writer of Ecclesiastes lived, the people observed regularly a popular festival named after a god, Adonis. Adonis was the deity of vegetation, especially of corn and wheat. Gardens of Adonis were carefully nurtured—baskets or pots in which wheat, barley, lettuce, and other crops were sown. When the plants began their growth, the baskets and their contents were flung into the sea. According to the pagan beliefs of that time, such offerings helped secure a good harvest.

Something of that notion, in a Christian setting, arises out of the Ecclesiastes passage. Cast your bread on the waters; realize some will be lost; but don't become too cautious with your deeds, and sooner or later the reward will be yours. "Cast your bread on the surface of the waters, for you will find it after many days" (Ecclesiastes 11:1, NAS).

The chief motivation for living ought not be reward. Yet the Bible clearly enunciates the fact that God does not overlook our acts of love. The writer of Hebrews said, "For God is not so unjust as to overlook your work and the love which you showed for his sake in serving the saints" (Hebrews 6:10, RSV).

Casting bread upon the waters is not done to receive rewards. But if in obedience to God the bread is cast, the reward ultimately comes.

Several weeks prior to the passing of the man I have mentioned in this chapter, I visited with his wife in their home. In astonishment I fingered through boxfuls of thank-you letters from people around the world who had been rescued from hunger by the works of this one dedicated man. The bread had already returned to him in this life.

The Old Testament Hebraic notion suggested that rewards for faithfulness necessarily came during one's earthly life. So we read: "He who is gracious to a poor man lends to the Lord, and He will repay him for his good deed" (Proverbs 19:17, NAS). That payment may or may not occur in this life, but the promise remains true. Throwing your bread into the world of need brings its eventual rewards. God has promised, and God does not lie.

Do you want to be as sufficiently prepared to die as possible? Do you want to be ushered out of this life with a measure of confidence and joy? The biblical recipe for such a graceful exit rests partially in the kind of life described by the wisdom writer: exert all the goodness you can muster, by the grace of God, and invest your energies in the lives of people. Recognize some of the "bread" will be lost. But let not the prospect of waste produce too much caution in your ministries of helpfulness. Then believe the promise of God: He is never so ungrateful as to forget your labors of love. He rewards.

14

Dismantling the Tent

My generation has become enamored with camping. Employers bemoan the eagerness of workers to drop their tasks on Friday afternoon to begin a weekend at the lake. The highways, crowded with camper trailers and trucks, are obstacle courses clogged by boats and camping equipment of every variety. For those less inclined to luxury, or unwilling to pay the price, a tent has become standard equipment in the American home.

Religious rituals in the Hebrew tradition virtually legislated that faithful Jewish families embrace the camping habit, too. Three annual festivals called for every able-bodied Hebrew within traveling distance to go to Jerusalem to celebrate.

The Feast of Tabernacles was one grand camping experience. The week-long ritual reminded the Jews of the years their fathers wandered in the wilderness, living in tents. During that week everyone moved into the streets and into makeshift housing—tents. Even Jerusalem residents joined their out-of-town cousins in the gigantic annual camping jamboree.

The tent was standard equipment in the Hebrew home. Camping gear rarely got rusty. It was utilized often, both by choice and by decree.

Some moderns have discovered, only after a substantial investment, that a tent or camper can become a liability. Once the freshness of roughing it has worn off, tenting may well lose its glamor. The Hebrews, too, accustomed to more substantial housing, may have looked upon the tent as, at best, a very temporary kind of shelter.

A tent symbolized impermanence. It required repeated setting up and pulling down. The tent was easy prey for wind and rain. It would suffice for a temporary home, but permanence was not one of its features.

When the Apostle Paul reflected upon life's struggles and the prospect of death, his mind focused on the familiar tent. He said to the Corinthians: "For we know that if the earthly tent which is our house is torn down, we have a building from God, a house not made with hands, eternal in the heavens" (2 Corinthians 5:1, NAS).

Anticipating Dismantling the Tent

The apostle, thinking seriously about the end of earthly life, looks forward with anticipation to shedding his physical body—the earthly tent. The prospect of a more permanent building—one constructed by God and lasting forever—strengthens his desire to be freed from the body he describes as a tent.

Human beings learn very quickly to love and protect and admire their fragile but marvelously constructed bodies. The young child's discovery of his hands is fascinating and thrilling, not only for the infant, but also for those who watch. The human body is, indeed, a fascinating bit of equipment, not only for the infant, but even more so for a mature adult.

When the body remains strong and comparatively free from ailments, it is easy to believe that we are fearfully and wonderfully made. And we come to love and cherish that body, however temporary and fragile and subject to disease it may be.

We fight to maintain our tent. We protect it from a thousand onslaughts. Fear multiplies into terror when we face prospects of losing this temporary dwelling place. While writing this chapter, I was interrupted by the tearful pleas for help from one who has endured intense grief very recently. Her doctor, after extensive examinations, has announced the presence of a tumor in her body. Her tent is threatened and she is afraid.

We can understand the elderly or terminally ill person who wishes to be relieved of this earthly tent. Living in a leaky, poorly sheltering tent no doubt encourages the desire to shed the physical body. When that body no longer is capable of doing what it has been made to do, shedding it may be preferable to remaining in it.

The apostle knew something about physical frailty. He struggled with an imperfect body. He resented but accepted his "thorn in the flesh." And he had concluded that God had prepared something preferable to living in the body. He was aware of a new, unfailing, eternal body. He was prepared— even gladly entertaining the prospect of giving up the body that had served him on earth.

Paul no doubt was influenced by Greek and Roman philosophers of his day. One particular, popular school of thought despised the human body. It was considered a tomb. Epictetus said of himself, "Thou art a poor soul burdened with a corpse." Seneca said, "I am a higher being and born for higher things than to be the slave of my body which I look upon as only a shackle put upon my freedom."

A proper reflection upon the body's role in our lives does not disdain the physical tent. It, rather, senses the freedom a new spiritual body will provide for us after death. The apostle was aware that the new, God-built house he would inherit would be capable of so many things now impossible. Rudyard Kipling may have sensed something similar when he wrote:

> When Earth's last picture is painted,
>   And the tubes are twisted and dried,
> When the oldest colors have faded,
>   And the youngest critic has died,
> We shall rest, and, faith, we shall need it—
>   Lie down for an eon or two,
> Till the Master of all good workmen
>   Shall put us to work anew.
>
> And those that were good will be happy:
>   They will sit in a golden chair;
> And splash at a ten-league canvas
>   With brushes of comet's hair;
> They shall find real saints to draw from—
>   Magdalene, Peter, and Paul,
> They shall work for an age at a sitting,
>   And never grow weary at all!
>
> And only the Master shall praise us,
>   And only the Master shall blame;
> And no one shall work for money,
>   And no one shall work for fame;
> But each for the joy of the working,
>   And each, in his separate star,
> Shall draw the thing as he sees it,
>   For the God of things as they are!

Kipling's theology may not pass our tests. Many of us

probably envision heaven as something different from a painting class. But the poet, like the apostle, anticipated the shedding of his earthly body. He was excited about the freedom his new tabernacle, a spiritual body, would possess.

Appreciating This Earthly Life

Paul's look was not confined only to the future. The flapping tent, temporary though it was, caused no depreciation of the body. He did not despise the tent. The apostle looked backward with appreciation to this earthly tabernacle—his physical body.

Men have frequently scorned their bodies, with dire results. The poet Francis Thompson at one point in his life disdained this earthly tent. He called it "vile corruption." Consequently, his life was crippled and shortened by a thoughtless abuse of the tent.

Looking forward to moving day, in Paul's thought, did not negate the value of the human body. He did not disparage this earthly life. He admitted frustration with his physical body. He groaned, longing to be clothed with his new body. But Paul looked upon this earthly tent—his physical body—as a gift of God to be held in honor.

In other writings the New Testament depicts our bodies as temples. Such edifices are respectable and often elaborate works of men. Our bodies, too, are wonderfully constructed and not to be disdained. Paul infers the value of the human body when he speaks of it as the residence of the Holy Spirit.

This present earthly life should not be downplayed because it houses the "arrabon," the first installment of the life to come. Because that initial installment, the Holy Spirit, has been granted to us, Paul insists on an earnest, productive life in this physical body. He urges his readers to live with courage, whether in this life or the next, saying,: "Therefore also we have as our ambition, whether at home or absent, to be pleasing to Him" (2 Corinthians 5:9, NAS).

Paul's persuasion is that the Christian can enjoy the best of two worlds. He can experience the foretaste of life ever-lasting while in this body. The first down payment of the af-terlife is already ours—the Holy Spirit's indwelling presence in our lives. Who then can disparage this temporary, flap-ping, storm-torn tent? It is God's gift and the promise of bet-ter things to come.

Christian believers too often conceive of God's promises being fulfilled only after death. That tendency is seen in the way we interpret Scripture. Paul quoted the Old Testament when he wrote: "Things which eye has not seen and ear has not heard, and which have not entered the heart of man, all that God has prepared for those who love Him" (1 Corin-thians 2:9, NAS). That is often interpreted as futuristic. However, the apostle was speaking of possible present experiences. We already possess the capacities for some of those wonders. The down payment of the Holy Spirit ener-gizes us so that we experience here and now, in our earthly tents, some of the glories of God. We dare not disdain the bodies that serve as the residence of that eternal Spirit.

Depreciating the human body cannot be harmonized with other directives in God's Word. We have been asked to "honor God in your body" (1 Corinthians 6:20, NEB). That can only mean that the earthly tabernacle is an instrument to be used for God's glory. A proper view of life includes ap-preciation for this earthly tent, fragile and weak as it may be.

Facing Soberly Prospects of Judgment

Any view of life and death is inadequate if it does not in-clude the aspect of ultimate judgment. Reward and punish-ment must be considered if life is to be lived under the lordship of Christ. The apostle was keenly aware of this judgment when he wrote: "For we must all appear before the judgment seat of Christ, that each one may be recompensed for his deeds *in the body,* according to what he has done, whether good or bad" (2 Corinthians 5:10, NAS).

That view of judgment was no morbid, foreboding anxiety about his future state. Paul anticipated the joys of the post-earthly life. He was aware, however, that other possibilities existed. He was a steward of his body.

Paul used the word *bema* for "judgment." The bema was the place of judgment. He was personally tried at the bema. In Greek trials jurymen were given two bronze disks. One was solid and the other hollow. They looked exactly alike on the outside. On the bema stood two vases or urns. One was bronze and was called the "decisive" urn because it was in this vase that the guilty or innocent verdicts were placed. At the trial's close, the jurymen dropped their disks into the urns—the hollow disk into the "decisive" urn if guilt was indicated, and the solid disk into the other vase if the decision was not guilty. Both disks appeared alike. No spectator knew how a juryman voted. The decision was known only after the judge counted the discs in the "decisive" urn.

Life is like that. We are casting our decisions. We do that by the kinds of lives we live. We do that in part by the deeds done in the body, this earthly tent. No man can convict or acquit us, but there is judgment coming. Paul recognized that and concluded that it should therefore be our ambition to be the kind of persons in whom God could find pleasure.

It is amazing to see the amount of decoration some people put on the tent of their earthly lives. They spend a lifetime amassing decorations and hangings for the earthly tent. What a folly it would be if a man fitted out a little tent on the backyard of a huge estate and hung it with priceless hangings. How incongruous to set up a tent and then put million-dollar paintings on the sides. What madness to do that and leave the mansion on the estate grounds empty except for dust and echoes.

Yet people practice that constantly. Men and women forget that judgment is coming. They lavish their resources upon this earthly body and its desires. They become poverty-stricken in spirit. Disregarding ultimate judgment, they live in this earthly tent as if it is their permanent home. They decorate that tent with costly paintings, not realizing that one day the stakes will be pulled from the ground, the tent will be folded, and judgment will follow.

The call for all who reflect seriously on the biblical view of death and life is to look forward to release from this earthly life, but to appreciate its temporary function as the vessel in which the Holy Spirit lives. The realization of its passing goodness, together with the prospect of judgment, motivates the believer to use his body and his whole earthly life in a manner pleasing to God.

15

Cultivating a Garden of Memory

Grandma Jost lived just three houses down the street. There was no blood relationship between us, but she was "Grandma" to our young daughter. Cookies and candy were always on hand when Holly and her little friends came to her house. In the beginning Grandma invited them in; often, I'm afraid, they simply walked in and waited for the handouts.

I personally walked by Grandma Jost's house at least four times a day and often more. But I passed by not for treats, but because she lived along the path I took in walking to the church daily.

I had often noticed something in her yard, almost hidden among the petunias and phlox, but not until she died did I contemplate the words I had seen so often. On a little, black, steel marker stuck into the ground amidst the flowers were these words:

> The kiss of the sun for pardon,
> The song of the birds for mirth;
> One is nearer God's heart in a garden
> Than anywhere else on earth.

Those words were a partial commentary on this woman's life. She loved her garden. She reveled in the miracle of growth in nature. She rarely was seen outside the house unless she was tending the multitude of growing plants around her house. Even when she became physically unable to plant and cultivate, the vegetables and flowers that were planted for her or came up perennially were a constant source of joy.

This elderly woman loved to visit. But her visits outside the home were almost always carried on with a hoe or hose in hand. She visited with her neighbors while she sprinkled her garden. She talked about the weather and the need for rain, while intermittently she chopped away at the disgusting weeds that invaded her little kingdom. When a heart condition didn't allow for outside activities any longer, the windowsills, replete with fragrant blossoming plants, were evidence that she would have her garden somewhere, so long as she would live. I really believe she was persuaded that . . .

> One is nearer God's heart in a garden
> Than anywhere else on earth.

The life of this grandmother and neighbor has provided the occasion for me to reflect upon how we view the faithful dead. My close relationship with her and the memories of her gardens have prompted me to think about how I need to deal with the memories of people I have loved and lost.

One of the priceless gifts God grants us is the garden of memories. Perhaps it is as necessary for us to cultivate such a garden of memories as it seemed necessary for this woman to nurture those flowers and vegetables. The garden of memory is something no one can rob from your life.

Shakespeare once put words in the mouth of Mark Antony that trouble me. In his oration over the body of the assassinated Caesar, Mark Antony said: "The evil that men do lives after them; the good is oft interred with their bones." There is truth in those lines. Evil deeds and evil men sometimes cast long and dark shadows. But it is not necessarily true that what good men do is buried with their bones. There can be gardens of memories that need never be buried.

The writer of Proverbs suggested this when he wrote, "The memory of the righteous is blessed" (Proverbs 10:7a, NAS). The writer of Revelation in the New Testament expressed a similar sentiment when he wrote, "Blessed are the dead who die in the Lord from now on! 'Yes,' says the Spirit, 'that they may rest from their labors, for their deeds follow with them' " (Revelation 14:13, NAS).

Fortunate is the family that can relax after paying their last tributes to a loved one and cultivate the garden of memory. The capacity to nurture such a garden means that you need never pay your last respects to a departed family member. The garden of memory keeps that respect alive and growing.

In the parsonage where we live is a Christmas cactus, usually hidden away in an unused bedroom where it is cool and sunny. More often than not the cactus produces beautiful, pink flowers during the holiday season. But that plant, ugly in some respects when it is not blooming, performs another function in our home. It came from the home of another of our neighbors. That woman has been dead for many years, but one simple cactus plant serves as a garden of memories that reminds us of pleasant associations with someone we learned to love.

One of the worst punishments that can come to us is the obliteration of memory. When the people of Israel wished the worst for their enemies, they spoke of erasing even the memory of their foes.

> They are dead, they will not live;
> They are shades, they will not arise;
> To that end thou hast visited them with destruction
> *And wiped out all remembrance of them.*
> —Isaiah 26:14, RSV, emphasis added.

One of the greatest blessings of the people of Israel was their recollections of a God who loved them. They set up stones so that this garden of memory would be nurtured. They composed poetry so that their history would not be forgotten throughout the coming generations. They knew something about the cultivation of gardens of memories.

Alex Haley spoke a few brief words at the close of the second showing of the television series "Roots." He encouraged people of all races to reach back into the past. He urged younger people to ask questions of their elders. He appealed for written records of family events. He proposed that more families ought to have reunions. He was urging a generation plagued with family rebellions instead of family reunions to give attention to the cultivation of gardens of memory.

What should you plant in a garden of memory? What are the seeds and bulbs that need to be planted if such a garden is to prosper and bear fruit? I have allowed my thoughts to linger on the life of that grandma who loved to garden. From her life I have made some observations about the contents of a garden of memory.

Families Are Blessings of God

Grandma Jost once took me to task as I hurried by her house. She didn't appreciate what I had said in the sermon the previous Sunday. I had spoken about children. I had suggested that in the "old days" children were a financial asset, because they could do the farm work. I went on to say, however, that today children were a financial liability. She hadn't understood everything I meant by that, but she was definitely perturbed. Children were a blessing of God, and she didn't want me to forget that.

She came from a large family. She knew what it was to enjoy the companionship of brothers and sisters when times were hard. She, too, had a rather large family. She saw each one of them as gifts from God. She wasn't about to allow her pastor to speak of children as liabilities without at least an opportunity for rebuttal.

She wasn't suggesting that children always provide joys and no sorrows. She was well aware of the hazards of child-rearing. She sometimes shared some of those unhappy experiences as I shuffled slowly past her house. But the unhappy moments with children did not dim her enthusiasm for children. She acknowledged and championed the cause of family life.

That's a good flower to nurture in our garden of memories. In an age of declining baby population, this flower isn't always that popular. When more couples deliberately determine not to bring offspring into the world, there may be danger of forgetting that family life is precious and God-ordained.

The Bible always speaks in affirmation of the family. The sacred relationship of Christ to the church is described in terms of family life. The body of Christ, the church, is repeatedly depicted as God's family. Family life does not grow outdated. It is a plant to be nurtured with great care.

Some of the saddest scenes witnessed by pastors is death in a family where relationships are strained or even antagonistic. Nothing makes the passing of a loved one more painful than the knowledge that there is an unfinished agenda within the family. On the other hand, nothing is more beautiful than a loving, unified family planning, reminiscing, working, and worshiping together when a mother or father has departed this life.

Tending the garden of memories demands strengthening family relationships. Working through grief in a healthy fashion is possible only when parental and sibling relationships have been pleasant. All too recently have I witnessed the agony of grieving hearts, not just because death has entered the family, but because something else had died earlier—loving relationships. Tending the garden of memories dictates that family members not let the sun go down on their wrath.

Families are blessings of God when they are bound tightly by strings of love. The weeds of discord and animosity incapacitate a family from reflecting properly upon death and life.

Prayerful Intercession Is Family Work

Children can walk through their gardens of memories so much more easily when they know they have been surrounded by praying parents. Children tread more softly and carefully through the flowers and ferns of their memory garden when they are assured that a mother or father's prayers have sanctified that garden.

That grandmother who loved her flowers loved her children as well. They did not always respond to her love as she hoped. She had her disappointments. She became frustrated with her children. They disobeyed. They refused her counsel at times. But she always continued to pray for them night and day. Her children knew that part of their heritage was a prayerful mother. It was difficult, perhaps, to see her ushered into heaven, but her life also provided a beautiful garden of memories that has strengthened them often since her death.

Jesus had His close friends. He had a family, even though He had few relatives. His relationship with His friends grew intensely stronger with the weeks and months and years. But the secret of His relationships with His spiritual family was His prayers for them. How often must the disciples have walked through their garden of memories after Jesus was not present physically. That garden was strewn and bathed with the Master's prayers.

Do you want your loved ones to meander in gardens of memories after you no longer remain with them? Do you want those memories to be most meaningful and never forgotten? Pray! Pray without ceasing. Prayerful intercession is family work.

Constructive Attitudes Are Essential to Healthy Gardens

One of the pitfalls of advancing age is the tendency to become pessimistic. An agonizing world makes it easy to become cynical and self-centered. The pains of the aging body rob you of energy that should be used for others. As the world rushes by, the older person may be tempted to be judgmental and critical. It is easy to see more of the weeds of the world than its flowers.

Chopping weeds demands far less skill than growing flowers. Tending a garden requires pruning and weeding and hoeing, but little skill is demanded for those chores. To nourish and encourage and cultivate and fertilize and transplant and thin is more exacting work.

Grandma Jost grieved often about one thing, the practice of some of criticizing the church. She was troubled when people were unloving and intolerant. She knew that things were not always as they should be. She did not always agree with the decisions of the church. But she would not stoop to bitterness and complaining. She lived in the Spirit of the Master who said that He had come to build up rather than destroy. She lived in the spirit of the man about whom the poet wrote:

> An old man, going a lone highway,
> Came at the evening, cold and gray,
> To a chasm, vast and deep and wide,
> Through which was flowing a sullen tide.
> The old man crossed in the twilight dim;
> The sullen stream had no fears for him;
> But he turned when safe on the other side
> And built a bridge to span the tide.
>
> "Old man," said a fellow pilgrim near,
> "You are wasting strength with building here;
> Your journey will end with the ending day;
> You never again must pass this way;
> You have crossed the chasm, deep and wide—
> Why build you the bridge at eventide?"
>
> The builder lifted his old gray head:
> "Good friend, in the path I have come," he said,
> "There followeth after me today
> A youth whose feet must pass this way.
> This chasm that has been naught to me
> To that fair-haired youth may a pitfall be.
> He, too, must cross in the twilight dim;
> Good friend, I am building the bridge for him."
>   —Will Allen Dromgoole

That's a good spirit to cultivate. It's delightful to walk in the garden of memories where you can recall the constructive attitudes of a departed loved one.

The memory of the righteous is blessed when the spirit of building-up has been evident. The memory of the just is delightful when we are aware that those preceding us to glory have been bridge-builders.

Someone has suggested that God has placed two wonderful lamps in our hands. One is the lamp of hope. That light leads us forward through the uncertain mists of the future. The other is the lamp of memory. That light takes us by the hand and leads us back through the mists of the past to the happy scenes and experiences of yesterday. The lamp of memory, when life has been lived constructively, provides many beautiful journeys through pleasant gardens. We owe such gardens of memory to those we leave behind.

16

Reserving Hasty Judgment

Life and death, through our finite human eyes, consist of a vast tangle of mystery and loneliness. Perhaps the epitome of such confusion plagues the believer's mind when suicide occurs. Questions overwhelm us in the natural deaths that occur and under the most normal conditions. However, when a person, especially a child of God, takes his own life, the questions become even more formidable, and the answers elude us. Neither the Bible nor our own thinking satisfy the gnawing, troubling queries of our minds in such situations.

Ellen de Kroon Stamps, former traveling companion of Corrie ten Boom, shares with her readers some of the agony associated with knowing that a loved one has taken his own life. In her book, *My Years with Corrie*, Ellen recounts the pain and guilt she felt about her own father's unfortunate death. As a little child she had been afraid when she realized her carpenter father worked on tops of tall buildings and might fall from the high beams above. Years later a hospital director informed her of her father's death. He did not fall from a high building as she had once feared. Life itself had become too high a building for him and he had become afraid to walk the beams. He had taken his own life.

Ellen Stamps confesses that for weeks she walked through a dreamland. Even years later she struggled with guilt feelings, thinking that perhaps she could have reached her father's hidden thoughts but hadn't. At other times resentment boiled inside of her.

The reader should not expect definitive answers in this chapter regarding the future state of those who choose to destroy their own lives. I only know that in my relationships with such people I have found them entangled in a maze of thoughts almost incomprehensible to most of us. I know, too, that Christians find it so difficult to reconcile self-destruction with biblical truth that they grasp at any straw for the slightest indication that the death may not have been self-inflicted.

The difficulty we have in dealing with suicides is also revealed in the curiosity of people not closely related to one who uses self-destruction as the means of escaping the unsolved problems in his life. At least three times I have officiated and preached at the memorial services of suicide victims. Each time my attention has been arrested by the curiosity of virtually uninvolved people. Some always attend such services to discover what the pastor will say. The question arises immediately in the minds of some: what can a minister of God say in the hour of trial to a family who stands confronted with the reality that a loved one chose a strange way to resolve the pressures of life?

On one such occasion God directed my attention to the passage in John 16, where Jesus spoke to His disciples about

His imminent departure. While no ready-made answers for
our basic questions about suicide arise from those words, I
have found them helpful as I ponder the biblical view of
death and life.

Knowledge at Best Is Incomplete

Final answers come quickly from some "wise" people
when suicide occurs in the community or church family.
Quick, ready, unbending answers slip off the tongues of
some. The passage in John 16, however, demonstrates that
the knowledge of people, at best, always remains incomplete. We do well to remember that. Jesus said to the disciples, as He prepared them for His death: "Don't jump to
hasty conclusions. Reserve your judgment. Don't condemn
too hastily."

What occasioned the words in John 16:29-33? The disciples experienced incomplete knowledge and once they
thought they understood something Jesus said, they rejoiced. Their ignorance reached its depths when Jesus spoke
about His coming death. But suddenly they sensed they had
discovered the secret. "Lo, now You are speaking plainly,
and are not using a figure of speech" (John 16:29, NAS). It
was their naive way of saying, "Now we know what You've
been trying to tell us. At last we've figured it all out."

Jesus responded in a fascinating manner. He said in effect: "You think you understand it now? Be careful! The
hour is coming, and indeed is already here, when you will
scatter. The doubts will reappear and you'll walk down your
Emmaus roads wondering how you could ever have been so
badly fooled." The twelve applauded themselves for finally
catching on, but Jesus broke into that premature self-
congratulation with a warning. He desired that they realize
that at best their knowledge was far from complete.

The Lord of life reminded His friends about becoming too confident in their knowledge. We need that reminder when we reflect upon the imponderables associated with self-destruction. At best our knowledge of death and life always remains incomplete.

In Bunyan's *Pilgrim's Progress* there is a time when the pilgrims get a bit over-excited about their progress and success. Bunyan then reminds them that they have not yet completed life's end. He suggests that times of testing and rivers to cross remain in the future. Don't jump to hasty conclusions! Reserve your judgment!

The disciples in Jesus' day needed such words. We need them, too. We need to hear the admonition: "Don't jump too quickly to conclusions that may be based on partial knowledge. You can run far and well and still stumble. A sin may be conquered, only to rise up again and regain dominion in your life." We possess incomplete knowledge. The consciousness of that partial knowledge ought to close our mouths when tempted to make harsh judgments.

Ellen Stamps learned, among other things, how true it was that she knew so little. She says: "I also realized that I had to leave Papa in the merciful hands of Jesus. I had to face the fact that I did not and could not know my father's heart. We can never know what goes on in the inner life of another person. It was not up to me to judge Papa's exact relationship with Jesus."°

Loneliness Is Our Chief Test

If anything drives a person into frantic fear, it is the thought of being utterly alone. Jesus experienced that sensa-

<hr />

°Ellen de Kroon Stamps, *My Years with Corrie* (Fleming H. Revell Company, 1978).

tion on the cross and cried out, "*My God, My God, Why hast
Thou forsaken Me?*" (Mark 15:34, NAS). No other test
exasperates and threatens the victim so much as the fear of
being alone. The disciples would know that loneliness after
the cross. The whole world would cave in upon them. The
absence of Jesus would force them into intolerable aloneness.

I sense from Jesus' words that these apparently knowl-
edgeable disciples would discover their utter helplessness in
finding themselves alone. "Behold, an hour is coming, and
has already come, for you to be scattered, each to his own
home, and to leave Me alone; and yet I am not alone, because the Father is with Me" (John 16:32, NAS). Jesus inferred in those words that His followers, too, would find
themselves alone. He would enjoy the fellowship with His
Father, but they would agonize in their separation from
Him.

The crisis would come for the Twelve. They would be
scattered, each to his own way. In the upper room with Jesus
they thought they understood the meaning of the cross and
Jesus' coming death. They felt strong and capable of bearing
whatever would come. But the day of solitariness had not yet
arrived. Their chief trial remained a future experience and
would consist primarily of being left alone.

When I ponder the deaths of those for whom life has become too high a building and they jump, I sense few
answers. Instead I recognize my lack of complete knowledge. I can never know the inner thoughts that preceded
self-destruction. I know little of the loneliness that such
persons endure. And knowing so little, I reserve judgment.

God Never Leaves Us
Jesus shared a confidence with the Twelve that He desires

to leave with us as well. He knew the disciples would run when He, their Leader, would be crucified and entombed. He knew that His death would scatter those whom He loved. He recognized they would forsake Him. But He longed to have them understand one thing: He would not be alone. "Yet I am not alone, because the Father is with Me" (John 16:32, NAS).

What Jesus had said to these soon-to-be-deserters a few hours earlier was that they, too, would not be left alone. He assured them they would not be orphaned (John 14). He promised not to leave them comfortless. The nature of God demands that He never leaves a man alone. So loyal was Jesus that if Simon Peter would deny Him, and Jesus knew full well that he would, even then the Lord would not forsake Peter.

There in that upper room the disciples were being prepared to disperse in ugly panic that could have insulted Jesus' leadership and teaching. Yet the Lord insisted that in such moments He would not forsake them. They could count on Him holding them in His heart.

I'm not certain what the truth of our Lord's faithfulness means in instances where men and women become unfaithful, despair of life, and destroy it. I only know that to such people and to those who remain, grieving and perplexed, our God is saying: "I know exactly what's going to happen. I am prepared to tell you how frightened and scattered you will be. You are going to be disloyal, but never imagine that your disloyalty will shock me. I know when it is coming, and it doesn't change my love for you. Don't despair. I will not leave you."

What about the loved one who has seen fit to end his life violently? I share with you all the nagging questions and frustrations of the human heart. But I also share with you the ringing announcement of Jesus that He never leaves us. Our unfaithfulness to Him does not sever His love for us. Our hope rests in His unfailing love.

> Come, ye disconsolate, where'er ye languish,
>   Come to the mercy-seat, fervently kneel;
> Here bring your wounded hearts, here tell your anguish;
>   Earth has no sorrows that heaven cannot heal.
>
> Joy of the desolate, light of the straying,
>   Hope of the penitent, fadeless and pure;
> Here speaks the Comforter, in mercy saying,
>   "Earth has no sorrow that heaven cannot cure."

—*Thomas Moore* and *Thomas Hastings*

17

Reflecting on Extended Life

Hezekiah, one of the better kings of Israel, became acutely ill. After fourteen years of reigning as ruler of God's people, he faced the prospect of death. Humanly speaking, recovery was impossible. One of his good friends, Isaiah, heard about this sad state of affairs. He rushed to Hezekiah's side. Hezekiah, a young man probably still in his thirties, had much he still wanted to accomplish. Hezekiah likely inquired of Isaiah about the prognosis: "Will I recover?" His friend truthfully answered that the king must die.

The Bible reports that Hezekiah turned his face to the wall and prayed. Doubtless, Isaiah prayed as well. And prayer won. God spared the king. Notwithstanding the correctness of the human diagnosis, a spiritual physician effected a physical cure. God granted Hezekiah a fifteen-year extension of life.

The remedy, interestingly enough, came not without the aid of existing medical supplies. Isaiah applied first aid and laid figs on the diseased spot. Isaiah carefully reminded the king that healing had come to him not primarily through the figs, but through God's loving mercy. But both prayer and the poultice effected the restoration of health. Medical aids were not unknown nor unused even in more primitive biblical times.

The conquests of modern scientific medicine force us to contemplate the meaning of extended lives. Most of us, living in an age of advanced medical technology, face the happy or unhappy prospect of living to a ripe old age. The average life span continues to rise as more older people are kept alive by miracle drugs. That prospect forces the Christian believer to reflect on the meaning of extended life. Hezekiah's experience contains lessons from which we can learn.

Extended Life Is a Gift

Several years ago I conducted a funeral service for a man who realized he had lived on borrowed time. He and his family believed strongly that God had granted him extra years. Like Hezekiah, through the goodness of God and the skills of doctors, he lived longer than he had expected. He accepted extended life as a gracious gift from God.

The conviction of prolonged life as a gift from a loving heavenly Father germinated many years before his death. When the family escaped out of Russia by way of what is now Turkey, circumstances delayed their journey nine months and they nearly starved to death. Only by the grace of God and food supplies from a relief agency did they arrive in America. God's deliverance, through grace and medical supplies and unexpected groceries, brought extended life.

On another occasion, when submitting to surgery, doctors questioned this man's ability to survive. Once again God saw fit, through prayer and the medical profession, to spare his life.

That man never failed to remind himself and his friends and family that his later years represented God's gift of life and strength. We do well to reflect on the fact that not only will many of us live longer than our forefathers; all of us live on borrowed time. "My times are in Thy hand" (Psalm 31:11, NAS), David reminded the people of God.

Accustomed to seeing people live into their eighties and nineties, we may come to believe that we deserve continued life. We can easily jump to the conclusion that God owes us a continued existence on this earth. The biblical view of death and life demands that we pause in the midst of the busyness of life to remind ourselves: "Every moment granted to me comes by the grace of God. I live on borrowed time. Life belongs to God. He sustains me."

Miraculous recoveries from illness or disease should not be required to remind us that God sustains life. Our ingenuity does not keep this body breathing and active, although our inventiveness no doubt affects longevity. We eat and drink to stay alive, but the Word of God stabs us awake to the fact that God sustains us. Hezekiah, having profited from the poultice of figs, was confronted with the fact that God, not simply the figs, was responsible for his extension of life.

Extended Life Demands Service

If God ordains that men and women live longer, a certain responsibility rests upon us. Extended life demands additional service. The popular notion abounds that increased time away from one's job (a shorter work week) means more time for recreation. Will we take the same approach in responding to extended or prolonged earthly existence? Does added life span simply give license for more years for leisure and withdrawing from the work God has entrusted to

His people? I hope not. Obviously, advanced age makes some forms of work impossible, but extended life creates the necessity for us to discover new forms of service equal to the strength we possess in those added years. Extended life demands extended service.

When Hezekiah received back his health and an extension of years, he wrote a poem. He spoke about how downcast he had been and how he had pled with God for deliverance from sickness. And then he proceeds to say:

> Yes, now I see it all—it was good for me to undergo this bitterness, for you have lovingly delivered me from death; you have forgiven all my sins. For dead men cannot praise you. They cannot be filled with hope and joy. The living, only the living, can praise you as I do today. One generation makes known your faithfulness to the next. Think of it! The Lord healed me! Every day of my life from now on I will sing my songs of praise in the Temple, accompanied by the orchestra. Isaiah 38:17-20, LB.

What motivated Hezekiah to ask for extended life? Oh, I'm confident he suffered from the normal fear of dying. But he also realized additional work remained to be done. The people and the land faced great trials. Hezekiah grieved for his people. Admittedly, mixed motives surely caused him to cry out for extended time on this earth, but he desired to work for the people of God.

Whenever we become recipients of extended life, through miraculous healing or the so-called normal miracles produced by modern medicine, we owe praise to God. Hezekiah vowed never to cease praising God in the temple. Our prolonged lives ought to issue out in vigorous thanksgiving and praise. But we cannot stop with praise. We must work. Service with renewed dedication becomes the appropriate response to extended life.

Added years enable us to serve the God we love. Prolonged life becomes meaningful as we allow others' burdens to become our burdens. Hezekiah accomplished great works after his healing. "It was Hezekiah who stopped the upper outlet of the waters of Gihon and directed them to the west side of the city of David. And Hezekiah prospered in all that he did" (2 Chronicles 32:30, NAS). His response to extended life thrust him even more wholeheartedly into God's service.

With all his goodness, Hezekiah nevertheless also revealed his humanity. He could forget. He became ungrateful. The day came when pride controlled his actions. The passage following the words quoted above reveal that the king fell to the temptation to take pride in the possessions God had granted him. He flaunted those possessions and his increasing wealth before the eyes of enemy rulers. Hezekiah suffered because he failed to recognize the benefits of extended life as gifts from God and designed for added service.

All too easily we can reap the mercies of God, resolve to serve Him, and then quickly forget that God's extended mercies come to us for purposes of service, not self-glory. God strengthens us for each day's task; it is not our own doing. To use His grace for our own self-gratification misappropriates His mercies. So we may live longer than our forebears! So what? The biblical answer is clear: so that we may serve God and God's people in a more resourceful manner and praise Him for the privilege of service.

Extended Life Demonstrates God's Power

Hezekiah's extension of life resulted from his confidence in God's power. Although not without doubts, he became persuaded about the ability of God to do the out of the or-

dinary. Following Isaiah's directions, Hezekiah boiled some
dry figs, made a paste of them, spread it on the boil, and he
recovered. But the king remained unimpressed. He said to
Isaiah:

> "Do a miracle to prove to me that the Lord will heal me and
> that I will be able to go to the Temple again three days from
> now." "All right, the Lord will give you a proof," Isaiah told
> him. "Do you want the shadow on the sundial to go forward
> ten points or backward ten points?" "The shadow always
> moves forward," Hezekiah replied; "make it go backward." 2
> Kings 20:8-10, LB.

The Lord intervened in nature, and the sun stood still.
What if God should intervene, supernaturally or through
scientific progress, and spare your life until you reached 100
years or beyond? This Old Testament warrior's experience
teaches me that extended life serves the purpose of producing the consciousness that ultimately God's power enables
us. Futility becomes our lot unless the empowerment of God
is present. Hezekiah, in his better moments, recognized that.
But during fifteen years of added life he also suffered
memory lapses. Turning the shadow back and forth, not an
impossible task for God, was not designed to create ecstatic
feelings in Hezekiah. The moving of the sun in one direction
or another represented God's attention-getter. He broke the
rules of nature to impress upon Hezekiah that He was a God
of power.

Hezekiah received two answers to prayers. Could he ever
forget that? And yet he forgot. He thoughtlessly misappro-
priated his extended years. He served self. Instead of
remaining humble and attributing his strength to God,
Hezekiah heaped glory on himself.

Miraculous deliverance or exceeding longevity does not
insure a grateful spirit. One person, when quizzed about the

secret of his old age, gives honor to God. Another, having reached a similar age, attributes his extended life to a daily dose of hard liquor, sheer determination, and the will to live. The latter literally takes credit for his long life. The biblical view of extended life sees every moment as a gift from God. Added years are intended to multiply our consciousness of God's power in the world. Our added years, if God wills to grant them to us, come not for purposes of self-indulgence. Long life only enhances the opportunities for praising God and proclaiming His power in the world.

I recall the man who twice had been granted a reprieve from death by a rather spectacular deliverance from illness. He readily admitted that God had extended his life. But when asked to testify to the power of God in his life, he boldly refused.

On the other hand, a woman in our congregation continues to sing the praises and power of God for a miraculous deliverance that occurred 40 years ago. When about to give birth to a child, she was stricken with pneumonia. Her condition worsened. Oxygen was administered to keep her alive. The prognosis of a specialist, called at a time when hope was almost gone, was that she had one chance in a thousand for survival. Soon after, while delirious, the woman gave birth to a son, who died a few hours later.

The struggle for life, however, continued. Other complications sapped the woman's strength and her condition deteriorated even more. She felt compelled to call on several ministers, on the basis of the command in James to call for the elders if one is sick, to pray over her for healing. She was anointed with oil, the ministers prayed, and the woman confesses that she really felt no different from before. A conviction grew, nevertheless, that God had extended her life. After further prayer with her family, she called the pastor on

Saturday and declared she had been healed and would attend the Sunday morning worship service the next day. She did! She gave public testimony to God's great power in her life. She continues to give witness to that power even today. She lives in the spirit taught by the Bible—extended life demonstrates God's power and the believer praises God for that divine energy.

18

Swifter Than a Weaver's Shuttle

Flossie, a middle-aged, educated, ex-schoolteacher, taught me all I ever learned about weaving on a loom. As a young college graduate, needing a job that would allow my income to catch up with educational expenses, I met Flossie in a mental hospital. Assigned to work in occupational therapy, I supervised, among other activities, the weaving projects of several dozen patients. I had scarcely even seen a loom, let alone operated one. I recognized immediately that the product was beautiful, but the process completely intimidated me. My first day at work convinced me I would fail dismally in my first occupational task.

But Flossie taught me weaving. The apparently endless and sometimes tangled mass of yarn always yielded to her skill and agility. Patiently she transferred that knowledge and skill to me, a frightened, green college graduate with majors in history and Bible. I discovered how to string the loom with yarn. I learned to coordinate the movement of my feet, as they pressed the various foot pedals, with the swift movement of the shuttle as it passed through the waiting cords. Flossie taught me to become a teacher of others.

Flossie herself was a patient in the hospital. Periodically, about every six weeks she entered a manic stage that demanded the strength of six grown men to control her. Today drugs would control behavior like Flossie's, but then it was simply a matter of waiting for time. Then she eventually relaxed and slipped back into a more depressed state of mind, and she was harmless. More than that, she was exceedingly helpful to me. Declared unfit for society, Flossie tutored this young country college graduate so that he could become a useful part of the program of therapy in the lives of mentally disturbed people.

Flossie's contribution to my life has never been forgotten. But on one occasion, while preparing for a memorial service of a man taken very suddenly in death, the memory of Flossie's influence upon my life catapulted before me once again. Reading from the Book of Job, I saw the words: "My days are swifter than a weaver's shuttle" (Job 7:6, NAS). I had almost forgotten about looms and shuttles, but not about Flossie. Her life had forced me to reflect often about life and the unfairness of it. Why should a beautiful, capable, loving woman like Flossie carry the burden that she bore?

But when I studied the words of Job, I began to reflect not only on life, but on death as well. I tried to picture Job and his experiences. I imagined the kind of life that compelled him to speak of life being swifter than a weaver's shuttle. That imagery, no doubt, arose out of his everyday experiences at home.

Very likely Job's wife often sat by the weaver's loom and personally made the clothes worn by her seven children and her husband. She may have been as skillful as Flossie. I can imagine Job watching his wife working at the loom, marveling at the swiftness with which she passed the shuttle back and forth across the warp of the weaver's web. The shuttle sped across the loom with lightning-like speed.

Then one day tragedy struck their home. Job, stricken with disease, found himself with a body that was reprehensible both to others and himself. He had been the most successful businessman in town. Now he was despised—his flesh worm-eaten, hardening into scabs, then breaking out again and again into festering sores. His friends tried to console him and only added to his misery. And in a moment of discouragement and bewilderment, Job cast his eyes on the weaving of his wife and said, "My days are swifter than a weaver's shuttle" (Job 7:6, NAS).

Flossie probably occupies a grave somewhere today. The looms with which she and I worked likely became junk many years ago. The world has changed immeasurably, but the picture of that shuttle and the loom remains in my memories and in my reflections about death and life.

A Symbol of the Shortness of Life

The weaver's shuttle speaks to us of the swiftness of days. Job asserted that God's allotment of time was too brief. That assertion, however, was mixed with the persuasion of life's labor being too constant and unremitting. He saw life as mixed bag. One moment he compared life to the swiftness of a weaver's shuttle and in the same breath he likened life to that of a hired man who slaves away for his wages, but finds sunset so far in the future. He saw life in terms of a slave who pants for the shade and wishes the evening would come.

The slowness with which time passed caused him to cry

out: "So am I allotted months of vanity, and nights of trouble are appointed me. When I lie down I say, 'When shall I arise?' But the night continues, and I am continually tossing until dawn" (Job 7:3, NAS). And in the same breath he blurts out words about life passing swifter than a weaver's shuttle. Physical pain makes nights and days appear to be endless. Job logically should have renewed his wish for death, but instead he clings desperately to the dreary and painful lot that is left to him. He complains about the swiftness of his days.

Such inconsistency proves true in the experiences of men and women everywhere. They call for death when deeply hurt, but when facing death they generally ask for a reprieve. Milton said in *Paradise Lost:*

> For who would lose,
> Though full of pain, this intellectual being,
> Those thoughts that wander through eternity,
> To perish rather, swallow'd up and lost
> In the wide womb of uncreated night?
> —Book II, 11. 146-50

When reflecting upon death and life we need to remember what contradictory feelings reside within us. The days drag along at less than a snail's pace. We don't prize the preciousness of those moments until they pass. And then life suddenly reveals itself as flying by like a weaver's shuttle. Seneca expressed this wisdom when he wrote, "The velocity of time is infinite, and is most apparent to those who look back." Most of us recognize the fleeting nature of life and time. Yet the prospect of death startles us when we realize how swiftly life passes like a weaver's shuttle.

Job found other ways of expressing the fleeting nature of time. "Now my days are swifter than a runner; they flee away, they see no good. They slip by like reed boats, like an eagle that swoops on its prey" (Job 9:25-26, NAS). On another occasion Job lamented, "Man, who is born of woman, is short-lived and full of turmoil. Like a flower he comes forth and withers. He also flees like a shadow and does not remain" (Job 14:1-2, NAS).

Swifter than a weaver's shuttle! Like a breath of air that stirs for a moment in the treetops, and ripples swiftly across the field of grain, life eludes us. The weaver's shuttle speaks to us of the swiftness of our days.

A Symbol of Daily Addition to Life

A spirit of dismay and gloom wells up within me when I see my wife begin knitting a sweater or afghan or other article that I know will take weeks and months to complete. The same feeling comes over me when I watch the women of our church working on a quilt that requires what seems to be millions of tiny stitches, each painstakingly made with a tiny needle. The same feeling of desperateness came over me in those days when I first learned how to weave on a loom. But the weaver's shuttle speaks of a daily addition to the web of life, and that becomes important as we reflect upon death and life.

Job, watching the weaver at the loom, saw that no garment was created instantaneously. His culture knew no "instant" clothes. Everything came slowly, but it came, nevertheless. Real genuine life comes in a similar fashion. We do not produce "instant" lives. Lives that please God demand time. Each day adds a thread to the web of life. Each day holds the capacity for good or evil, for sin or holiness. Each day serves as another thread in the pattern of life woven by each of us.

If the weaver's shuttle serves as our teacher, we will recognize that we weave our life daily. The shuttle never ceases to move back and forth. Development of character never hangs in limbo. The pattern of our life constantly continues to be formed. The weaving continues even when our bodies become frail and less capable of vigorous activities. Perhaps the more intricate details are even formed in those difficult, unwelcome days. But the shuttle continues to move across the web of life.

Death stops the weaver's shuttle. It no longer speeds through the loom of this earthen body. That realization demands that we follow the counsel of the psalmist, "So teach us to number our days, that we may present to Thee a heart of wisdom" (Psalm 90:12, NAS). The psalmist calls for a carefully woven life in view of the shortness of our days. If our lives pass as swiftly as the weaver's shuttle, then the demand for careful patterning of our lives after Christ's life becomes all the more essential. Every day we add a little more to that pattern.

> Lord, when Thou seest that my work is done,
> Let me not linger on,
> With failing powers,
> Adown the weary hours—
> A workless worker in a world of work.
> But, with a word,
> Just bid me home,
> And I will come
> Right gladly—
> Yea, right gladly
> Will I come.
>   —*John Oxenham*

As much as we would like, God does not always see fit to call us home when we discover ourselves workless workers in a world of work. But we never determine when the handicraft on the loom is finished. God reserves that prerogative.

God asks us to make certain that we add the threads that will allow Him to weave a beautiful character. That happens day by day. The weaver's shuttle speaks to us of a daily addition to the web of life.

A Symbol of Unfinished Tasks

The weaver's shuttle speaks to us of an unfinished task. In those bygone days of mental hospital work, almost every evening my students and I left unfinished work on the looms. Viewing a finished product always brought gratification, especially to those patients whose self-image was quite inadequate. To view a completed rug, even with its defects resulting from inexperience and mistakes, caused a sense of exhilaration. But the process of weaving consumed the major portion of time.

In reflecting upon Job's statement about the swiftness of life, I have pondered what must have pained him most. Hurting intensely, what motivated him to desire longer life? Job knew a measure of success surpassing that of most of his peers. God rewarded his hard and faithful work with prosperity. A reputation for being honest, wise, and God-fearing prevailed in his home community. Why call for added years?

Job knew of other tasks that lay unfinished. Other ambitions waited fulfillment. And now his lifetime seemed so short. He wanted more time as life swiftly fled away. So he referred to his days as flying more swiftly than the weaver's shuttle.

In a very real sense every Christian believer leaves this life with unfinished work. Our earthly life is the process, not the end result—like an unfinished rug on the loom, waiting the day of completion. Even our best days on earth remain imperfect and incomplete.

The Bible teaches us, however, that the Christian continues his chief vocation in heaven. To serve and honor Christ becomes our chief ambition here; to serve and honor Christ will be our eternal privilege in the world to come.

I once enjoyed the fellowship and service of a deacon whose native skills never attracted a great deal of attention. He was a simple but successful farmer the major portion of his life. Retirement and advancing age forced him to reduce the amount of activity in his life. But often I discovered that in his "deaconing" he sought out needs other people overlooked. In his plain ways he ministered to people whose pains and anxieties escaped the notice of other deacons. The church had set him aside as a servant.

Literally translated, to "deacon" means to serve. Without being asked, this simple man carried out his servant-role. But he always felt inadequate for his tasks. He never considered his work completed. But I rejoice today to know that he continues to deacon. His servanthood only found a new arena. For the Bible teaches us that deaconing becomes the full-time occupation of God's children in heaven. The Word of God speaks of those who have gone to be with the Lord as having "washed their robes and made them white in the blood of the Lamb. For this reason, they are before the throne of God; and they *serve* Him day and night in His temple" (Revelation 7:14b-15a, NAS).

The chief vocation in heaven consists in deaconing, to serve Christ. The weaving of a life characterized by service continues forever and ever in the world to come. Yes, life passes more swiftly than a weaver's shuttle. But day by day we form the web that prepares us for the life to come. And applying our hearts to wisdom while we serve God and our fellowmen, we qualify for the supreme task of heaven—serving Christ night and day.

19

Dying with Undimmed Vision and Unabated Strength

While most of us want to live, many people pray that they can die. Our retirement centers are crowded with people, some of whom see no further reason for living. They cry to God to be taken home. Very often that longing to be with the Lord is not simply the consequence of a very mature view of death and life. Sometimes it is the fading sight brought on by glaucoma or cataracts that produces the feeling of uselessness and the desire to depart from this life.

For others the loss of hearing and the inability to enter into or enjoy conversations with others ushers in this deep longing to be relieved of life in this world. For many people the simple agonies of old age emphasize the truth of Paul's words that "to depart and be with Christ ... is very much better" (Philippians 1:23, NAS).

Aggravating the problem for those people who would rather depart is the realization that life is unfair. People much younger than they, and much more useful, humanly speaking, are suddenly snatched from this life, leaving so much work unfinished.

Recently I officiated at the memorial service for a middle-aged optometrist who was very active in the community and church. He had initiated a unique program of help to impoverished, sightless people in many of the islands and countries to the south of the United States. He died very suddenly and unexpectedly. His mother has told me often how she wishes she could die. She believes she is more than a century old, which is not quite true, but she justifiably feels that whatever contributions she can make to society are past. She eagerly looks forward to death, but instead her son has passed from the scene.

When we reflect upon death and life from God's point of view, we cannot avoid the problem of death for those who exit this life in the prime of life. How does a loving Father in heaven, with His wisdom and insight, reconcile the fact that the young die so prematurely? Apparently His views are different from ours.

When the Old Testament closes the final chapter of Moses' life, it does so with a strange observation. That observation can help us reflect on death through the eyes of God. In Deuteronomy 34 the writer states that Moses died and was buried in an unidentified place. The writer then says, "Although Moses was one hundred and twenty years old when he died, his eye was not dim, nor his vigor abated" (Deuteronomy 34:7, NAS).

Human reasoning might suggest that Moses wasn't a fit candidate for death. His continuing usefulness was not in question. We may explain that he had to die because of disobedience. Striking a rock, rather than speaking to it, prevented him from accompanying the people of Israel into the Promised Land. But he died a strong, active man. He had no need for an optometrist, even if there had been such. He had maintained 20-20 vision throughout his life. His strength never diminished. From our point of view he was too young to die. He should have lived. We do well to reflect on Moses' experience through the all-knowing eyes of God.

Moses' Death Came While Active

Advancing age and dimness of vision so often go hand in hand. Diminishing strength is still another symptom of growing older. I need only to observe my ninety-year-old mother-in-law groping around any room outside of the one small retirement center room she calls home to see how dimness of sight becomes a handicap of old age. Moses never had that experience. "His eye was not dim" (Deuteronomy 34:7, NAS). He was removed from the scene of earthly existence while in a very active stage, even though he was 120 years old.

Relatively few people are suddenly ushered out of this life, never experiencing the pain of being forced to retire. Modern medical practices sustain life long after profitable work is possible. Few escape the feeling of uselessness, dimming of vision and abatement of strength. In fact, we find ourselves pressed between two sides of a vise—we don't want to grow old and feeble and mentally incompetent, but neither do we want to die young. Possibly no sentiment is expressed more often to a pastor than this: "I hope I won't have to live so long that I won't be responsible or able to care for myself. I don't want to live if I am not mentally alert." Yet the only alternative in many cases is death before we really want to bid farewell to our loved ones.

Moses was a privileged man. He was both aged (as we understand old age) and strong. But in spite of his undimmed sight and undiminished strength, God saw fit to relieve him of his earthly responsibilities. He died as an active vigorous servant of God.

Moses' death portrays the dilemma created by those among us who are cut off very abruptly from this life. His sudden passing provides a commentary for us as we reflect upon the death of the young man who is crushed beneath a pile of rubble. Moses' untimely departure serves as a lesson for us as we contemplate the unfairness of "premature" deaths. Moses' exit speaks to the case of the 24-year-old mother who gave birth to a healthy baby boy and the following day died from a ruptured aorta. Moses' departure in strength is a lesson for all those unanticipated deaths that come when strength is not abated and eyesight is undimmed.

Those so-called tragedies may, indeed, be God's gifts reserved for a relatively small group of people. Few of us would choose to join that select group. But those who die in their prime years belong to an elite club that is reserved for only a few of God's people. In Genesis we read an interesting account of the death of Enoch: "And Enoch walked with God; and he was not, for God took him" (Genesis 5:24, NAS). That sounds like an abbreviated obituary for a heart attack victim. Enoch never experienced the diminishment of strength so typical of many who die in their prime.

The prophet Elijah was a similarly privileged servant of God. He evidently had some indication that his earthly exit was imminent. So he spoke privately and earnestly with young Elisha, who would succeed him. Elijah performed his last miracle by dividing the waters of the Jordan so he and Elisha could cross on dry land. Then he asked Elisha what the younger man would desire most as a parting gift. Then we read: "As they were going along and talking, that behold, there appeared a chariot of fire and horses of fire which

separated the two of them. And Elijah went up by a whirlwind to heaven" (2 Kings 2:11, NAS).

That must have been a deeply disturbing experience for
those who remained behind. The story tells us that Elisha
cried out after Elijah, but it didn't matter. The man of God
was gone. How often that is the story in our lives. The hale
and hearty are snatched from us. We cry out after them, but
to no avail. Their earthly life is spent. They die—like
Moses—in full vigor, active, and needed by many of their
friends. But they are gone.

Moses' Death Didn't End God's Work

The departure of Moses did not mean the end of the work
he began. Moses was a deliverer. He redeemed his enslaved
brothers and sisters. He had left the courts and comforts of
the palace to struggle against Pharaoh and Egypt for the
sake of his countrymen. He rescued people from captivity
and hardship. He led them, by way of a 40-year detour, to
the land flowing with milk and honey. It was a gigantic un-
dertaking, freeing people from lives of misery and pain.
Moses was a hero.

The account of Moses' death, however, makes it clear that
God's work did not die with Moses. After the writer speaks
of Moses' undimmed sight and unabated vigor, he follows
with the words: "Now Joshua the son of Nun was filled with
the spirit of wisdom, for Moses had laid his hands on him;
and the sons of Israel listened to him and did as the Lord
had commanded Moses" (Deuteronomy 34:9, NAS). God
supplied and prepared a successor to Moses.

We are often tempted to think that the absence of key
people means the end of certain ideas and enterprises.
Sometimes I suppose that is true. The Bible teaches us,
however, that God's work will not be thwarted. He always

provides a successor to carry the torch when it is dropped by someone whose life comes to an abrupt conclusion.

When I reflect on death and life through the eyes of God, I think I hear Him say when someone passes so quickly and prematurely from our midst: "Be assured that My work, if in reality it is My work, will not go down with one man. My kingdom cannot be thwarted. I may lose the best man I could have chosen, but the work will continue."

It is interesting to read the verse that follows after the reins of leadership have been turned over to young Elisha: "Since then no prophet has risen in Israel like Moses, whom the Lord knew face to face" (Deuteronomy 34:10, NAS). A giant had fallen. No one as great as Moses was available to replace him, but that didn't bother God. Moses' absence, great as he was, did not mean God's work would wither and die.

There is a passage in Genesis 5, where the death of Enoch is recorded, that at first glance looks like nothing more than a dull, boring, monotonous geneaology. We read there about Enoch's death. In rapid succession there are reports of the deaths of Enoch's son, Methuselah; and his son, Lamech; and his son, Noah. But those words should not be interpreted as boring geneaology. This is God's way of saying, "I use men and women. I need them desperately, but I am not bound nor confined to one person. I will work out My plan for the ages and it will not be frustrated. Even death cannot sidetrack Me from bringing salvation to the world."

We are not always capable of determining which of the works of men are of eternal value. Sometimes we no doubt place false values on temporal and transient programs. But one thing is certain as we reflect on God's view of death and life: one person's departure from this life does not spell doom. The drama of God's work never ends because one of His actors passes off the scene. The drama continues and will come to its rightful culmination. When the curtain falls on a life that we have come to love very dearly, we can be assured that the curtain on God's redeeming plan for the world will not fall until it is finished.

Moses' Death Was Homecoming

Moses cherished grand dreams for Israel. Those dreams had their embryonic beginnings back in the comfort of Pharaoh's palace. His visions for his people caused him to do rash things early in his ministry. He boldly set about to create justice and equality, even murdering to achieve his ends. In spite of this lifelong effort, his dreams were not all realized when he died. He was particularly saddened when God explained that he would not have the joy of setting foot on the Promised Land. He could only gaze from a distance.

The Lord said, "This is the land which I swore to Abraham, Isaac, and Jacob, saying, 'I will give it to your descendants'; I have let you see it with your eyes, but you shall not go over there" (Deuteronomy 34:4, NAS). Moses struggled inwardly in accepting that verdict from God. He would remain one step away from the fulfillment of his lifelong dream. And with that sadness in his heart he departed this life.

Moses had looked forward eagerly to Canaan as a new and better home. Who wouldn't have been looking with anticipation toward a new home after wandering in the wilderness for forty years? But God said: "While you haven't finished all you'd like to do, I am taking you home. That will be far better than the Promised Land called Canaan."

The optometrist I referred to earlier in this chapter kept some tapes in his car. The day following his death the family examined the tapes left in the car. They found one that he apparently had used last. The first song on that eight-track tape is one written by B. J. Thomas. It was probably one of the last songs to which the eye doctor listened. It was especially appropriate since the optometrist died in his sleep.

They say that heaven's pretty,
And livin' here is, too;
But if they said that I would have to choose between the two,
I'd go home—goin' home—where I belong.

Sometimes when I'm dreamin',
It comes as no surprise
That if you look and see that homesick feelin' in my eyes,
I'm goin' home—I'm goin' home—where I belong.

While I'm here I'll serve Him gladly
And sing Him all these songs:
I'm here, but not for long.

When I'm feelin' lonely
And when I'm feelin' blue,
It's such a joy to know that I am only passin' through;
I'm headed home—I'm goin' home—where I belong.

One day I'll be sleepin'
When death knocks on my door;
And I'll awake to find that I'm not homesick anymore,
'Cause I'll be home—I'll be home—where I belong.°

Death is not pleasant, but when seen from God's point of view it is life. It is homecoming. Death ushers us into heaven—where we belong.

Shadows of trials and even death will darken our paths. In such moments we do well to remember to rejoice in the vigor God gives us, even if life is snatched away in the midst of strength and youthful energy. We need to praise God that no good work ceases with one person's passing. We need to exult in the truth that for the believing child of God death is coming home—where we belong.

20

Home at Last

William Penner moved few mountains in his lifetime. Local merchants did not close their shops during the hour of his funeral service. He lived quietly and humbly. At the memorial service, a song was sung for which he had written both words and music. That day in 1974 may be the last time the song will ever be sung, but it expressed what one saint of God felt and recorded one day.

> There is a better home above,
> Where we shall dwell in perfect love.
> There the redeemed adore the King,
> The heavens with their praises ring.
>
> No threat'ning clouds can hide the sky
> Where the redeemed shall never die.
> The stream of life is flowing there,
> His everlasting glory share.
>
> The weary wand'rer there finds rest,

And sweet communion with the blest.
And soon the glorious day will come
And we shall reach our heavenly home.

There all our loved ones we shall meet,
Saints of all ages we shall greet.
All earthly things have passed away
And we shall be with Christ for aye.

At the close of three of the four scores of the last stanza, the writer had added the words: "Home at last! Home at last!"

That hymn likely will never appear in a hymnal and the selection may be closer to doggerel rather than poetic verse. But they are words that echoed the thoughts of one of God's children about death and heaven. And they were written almost 30 years before those words became reality for him.

When reflecting on the biblical view of death, we cannot escape the fact that the believer's exit from this life is viewed as going home. Jesus, addressing His closest friends on the eve of His death, said: "In My Father's house are many dwelling places; if it were not so, I would have told you; for I go to prepare a place for you. And if I go and prepare a place for you, I will come again, and receive you to Myself; that where I am, there you may be also" (John 14:2-3, NAS). Jesus inferred that our departure means coming home— home at last!

Home Represents Absence of Strangeness

Home at last is a place where we feel comfortable, not ill at ease. The difference between someone else's home and ours is that in the latter we sense no strangeness. Relaxation and relief are among the benefits of home. Most of us prefer home to a stranger's house.

When Jesus spoke about preparing dwelling places or

homes for His followers, He was speaking about heaven. But heaven was an unknown place for the disciples. His friends, like most of us, feared the strange and unknown. Even something as grand as heaven was not welcomed by these early believers if it meant surrendering the familiar surroundings of their earthly homes.

Jesus struggled to interpret heaven for His friends. How do you translate into words something that is indescribable and has never been seen? Jesus chose to use the picture of home. Heaven is going home.

It is difficult to see dying and leaving the familiar environment of this world as going home. Dying is strange. We've never done it before. It's always unrehearsed. No one has returned from the experience to share with us how pleasant and homelike it is. So death and the promised heaven intimidate us. They elicit strange emotions within us. Strangeness and home don't go together. So how can death mean going home? Home is the one place in the world where we do not expect to feel strange.

Yet Jesus felt that "home" was the best way to describe heaven. He assured us that this unknown, never-experienced place called heaven will not feel strange. It will be home—at last! William E. Brooks said of Jesus' use of this picture:

> He could have chosen no livelier word as symbol. What memories the words stir in us! It may have been only a humble house on a little street or a cottage down a country lane. But it held what the heart desires above all else, sympathy and understanding and welcome. To the boy away at school or in the foxhole, or to the man or woman anxious amid the tasks the years have brought, it tells of a place where problems are left behind and wounds are healed. Some day there would come the turning of the last corner, and then the mounting of the steps to the door that opened with the touch. And there would be light be-

yond the door and a mother's kiss and the warm clasp of a father's hand. Home—at last!°

The biblical view of dying and heaven is not that of strangeness, even though we have never experienced either of them. Dying and going to heaven is like going home. Home is not strange; it is a place where we will feel most at ease.

What a delight to flop down in my easy chair or on the family room rug after a busy day dealing with people—some of them strangers, and none of them my immediate family members. What a relief to settle down beside a glowing fire, throw off my shoes, grab the morning paper or watch the evening news. Heaven will be much better than that.

Home Represents an Arena for Growth

Home at last will be a place where we continue to grow, not stagnate. The New Testament provides only glimpses of heaven. Jesus is preparing a home for us. As I reflect upon the symbol of home as heaven, I sense there is much more substance in that picture than I can ever know in this life. What are the purposes of a home? Why do we live in homes?

Ideally, our home is a place suited particularly and uniquely to our individual characters. Heaven will not be a grand series of condominium apartments, every one just like the other. The dwelling place God is preparing for us will be adapted to our own, unique needs.

We have friends who recently purchased property in the desert for a future home. If and when that house is built, it

---

°Charles L. Wallis, Editor, *The Funeral Encyclopedia* (New York: Harper & Brothers, 1953), p. 64.

will be like no other house ever built. The site has been chosen to meet certain needs and provide special views. The topography has entered into the choice of that plot because their likes and dispositions call for specific specifications in that house. They may live in that house in their retirement years, but it will be so designed that they can pursue the hobbies and interests that will enable them to continue growing.

I picture the Savior planning and building a home for me in much the same fashion, but with superior wisdom and skill. I have no special insights about heaven, but I believe Jesus is preparing a place where I shall have the continual delight of knowing that I am growing.

There will be nothing "status quo" about heaven. The prepared mansions represent no environment where we remain the same forever and ever. Appetites for which we find no food here on earth will be royally satisfied in heaven. Dreams that appeared like vague outlines here will become realities in heaven. The rough visions of things we hoped for on earth shall be real there. And there will always be more in heaven. Stagnation will find no place in God's prepared place.

This note of growth, busyness, and serving is expressed in these lines:

> No, not cold beneath the grasses,
>   Not close-walled within the tomb;
> Rather in my father's mansion,
>   LIVING, in another room.
>
> Living, like the one who loves me,
>   Like yon child with cheeks abloom
> Out of sight, at desk or schoolbook,
>   BUSY, in another room.

Nearer than the youth whom fortune
  Beckons where the strange lands loom;
Just behind the hanging curtain,
  SERVING in another room.

Shall I doubt my Father's mercy?
  Shall I think of death as doom,
Or the stepping o'er the threshold
  To a bigger, brighter room?

Shall I blame my Father's wisdom?
  Shall I sit enswathed in gloom,
When I know my love is happy
  WAITING in another room?
                              —Robert Freeman

Home at last will never know inactivity. Home at last will be a place of continuing growth. It will be a place to live and serve and grow.

Home Is Where We Are Led

Home at last represents an event and a place to which we are led, not sent. Some of us recall our first day of school. For years we could hardly accept the fact we were too young to attend school. But when that day finally arrived, we were entering an unknown world. We looked forward to school eagerly, but there was fear, nevertheless. And if our parents were wise, they took us to school; they did not send us.

Death too often is portrayed as one experience that has to happen in isolation. No one can take that journey with us. An old song says, "There's nobody else can walk it for you; you've got to walk it by yourself."

Such a concept of dying is enough to frighten anyone. We enjoy traveling to familiar places in the company of friends. To journey to an unknown destination in complete aloneness strikes terror into our hearts. But the biblical view of death is that the believer does not make that trip alone or unaccompanied.

The psalmist reassures us when he says: "My God in His lovingkindness will meet me" (Psalm 59:10). Someone has suggested that the meaning of this expression is that our loving Father will meet us at every corner.

Death is not a road we travel by ourselves if we are Christians. There is One who has traveled that road ahead of us. And He has said He will travel it with us. You don't have to walk it alone. The God of mercy, as some translators have put it, will meet us at every corner.

My wife and I once arrived in Osaka, Japan, expecting to be met by a missionary couple. An error in their datebook left us without a reception committee. They were planning to meet us the following day. We knew other friends in Osaka, but we had no telephone numbers. The unusually kind and hospitable Japanese maidens at the airport wanted desperately to assist us. We spoke no Japanese and they understood almost no English. For several hours we were stranded feeling out of place and alone.

Death for the Christian holds no such prospects. We shall be led. God will guide us. We will be escorted, not sent without a guide. Anna L. Waring has expressed this idea so appropriately in a poem that has been set to music:

> In heavenly love abiding,
>   No change my heart shall fear,
> And safe in such confiding,
>   For nothing changes here.
> The storm may roar without me,
>   My heart may low be laid;
> But God is round about me,
>   And can I be dismayed?

Wherever He may guide me,
  No want shall turn me back;
My Shepherd is beside me,
  And nothing can I lack.
His wisdom ever waketh,
  His sight is never dim;
He knows the way He taketh,
  And I will walk with Him.

Green pastures are before me,
  Which yet I have not seen;
Bright skies will soon be o'er me,
  Where the dark clouds have been.
My hope I cannot measure,
  The path to life is free;
My Savior has my treasure,
  And He will walk with me.

21

Poetic Reflections on Death and Life

A husband and father died unexpectedly in his sleep. A daughter-in-law found herself terribly emotionally involved. She loved her husband's father dearly. She had been subjected to great trials in her life. She came from a broken home, but knew the love of a devoted blind mother. Three days after the death of her father-in-law, Val was scheduled to sing in a cantata written by John W. Petersen entitled "Jesus Is Coming." Should she sing as planned, including a solo part? Or could she sing, knowing the feelings in her heart? She decided to sing. Among the words sung were these:

> With the sound of trumpets announcing from the sky:
> Jesus is coming from heaven on high!
> See, now the pearly gates are open, Christ is passing,
> All the universe is watching as the King,
> Our Savior King descends to take His throne!
> With the sound of trumpets; triumphant is the song!

> Jesus is coming to right ev'ry wrong—
> Climax of history awaited so long!°

The basis for Petersen's words come from another hymn found in 1 Corinthians 15. The words of Paul in that passage probably appear to be prose, not poetry. But poetry they are! One of the reasons men compose poetry stems from the fact that they deal with things that defy language and baffle expression. Poetry enables the writer to use liberties not possible when writing a factual account for the daily newspaper. The "resurrection chapter" of 1 Corinthians 15 qualifies as poetry because it describes the indescribable.

The Apostle Paul, beseiged with questions by a troubled church in Corinth and hard-pressed to answer those queries, responded with poetry. He spoke strange words and difficult words! He reflected on corruption and incorruption, time and timelessness, death and victory, death and resurrection. He suggested these concepts moved beyond the comprehension of all but the "initiated."

> Brothers, I say this, that flesh and blood cannot inherit the Kingdom of God, nor can corruption inherit incorruption. Look now—I tell you something which only the uninitiated can understand. We shall not all die, but we shall all be changed, in a moment of time, in the twinkling of an eye, at the last trumpet. 1 Corinthians 15:50-52a, William Barclay.

I read those words often at funeral services, particularly at gravesides, and still I find them perplexing. They speak of truths that, even for the initiated, remain puzzling. Since the apostle used these words as instructions for those bewildered and confused, we do well to ponder them as we reflect upon death and life.

Unfit to Inherit the Kingdom

No man possesses the physical equipment entitling him to entrance into heaven. The most marvelously structured human body falls short of qualifying for entrance into that kingdom. God endows some with beautiful bodies. The intricacy with which our bodies function forces us to stand back in awe and amazement. The harmony with which the various organs cooperate as a human symphony never ceases to amaze the thoughtful person. The manner in which individual parts of the body rush to the aid of ailing members astounds us. We are, indeed, fearfully and wonderfully made.

But no one in his earthly body stands fit to inherit what God envisions for us ultimately. "An earthly body made of flesh and blood cannot get into God's kingdom" (1 Corinthians 15:50, LB). The best equipped person in the world for this life's tasks finds himself a pauper in terms of being outfitted for the next world. The strongest, most Charles Atlas-like body possesses nothing that gains him entrance into the kingdom.

Our bodies disintegrate in this life. Corruptible bodies do not qualify for the kingdom. Paul suggests later in this passage that mortality (the proneness to die) must be replaced with immortality. Earthly bodies must be transformed into heavenly bodies. Eternity accepts nothing that is corruptible. Heaven rejects the temporary or transient. There isn't room in God's heaven for anything that doesn't last forever.

Persons may sing well enough to make a joyful noise or even a very pleasant sound in the church choir, but that doesn't qualify them for the Metropolitan Opera. And even if you were a Beverly Sills and appeared regularly at the "Met," you would still lack the essential qualities necessary to join the choirs of heaven. Something has to change. These present bodies are not fit for the kingdom.

The ablest person who speaks and thinks and understands great truths still falls short of qualifying for heaven. No eminent scholar, endowed with superior intelligence, gains eligibility for heaven. No one is fit for the kingdom in this present body.

When we reflect upon death, the unfitness of our bodies for heaven ought to create in us a growing desire for change. Who desires to live forever, if this earthly body remains the "house" in which life carries on? Who would desire to be perpetually bound to this body throughout eternity? We really wouldn't want to live in these frail, mortal bodies forever. The prospect of living eternally in our human bodies holds no pleasant future for the thoughtful person. So it is imperative, as Paul suggests: "But I am telling you this strange and wonderful secret; we shall not all die, but we shall all be given new bodies! It will all happen in a moment, in the twinkling of an eye, when the last trumpet is blown" (1 Corinthians 15:51-52, LB).

No Need to Fear Death's Change

Sensible reasoning would indicate that, after suffering the hazards inherent in those physical bodies, we should welcome the change promised in the Word of God. Who would not exchange the tent of this earthly body for the temple of the heavenly? After watching life slowly ooze out of a terminally ill patient in the hospital over a period of weeks and months, should not the prospect of an incorruptible body appeal to our senses? And yet we steadfastly resist that exchange.

Even our bodies are so constructed that they resist death. How often that poor, frail, corpse-like organism called the human body persists in living when everything dictates that death prevails. The body, fragile as it appears, nevertheless possesses resiliency and the power to fight back that surprises us no end.

So our physical impulses and our emotional feelings combine to resist the thought of exchanging a worn-out body for an imperishable one. We fear the change because we almost always suspect change. The prospect of the unknown paralyzes us. Walking through the valley of the shadow of death strikes terror into our beings because we have never walked that path before.

The fear of death has always haunted men. When one person suggested boldly that he no longer feared the specter of death, a great man of God responded: "I have never had a moment in which death was not terrible to me." Those were not the words of an unbeliever. They reflected the honest thoughts of a child of God. Most of us share that fear.

The Apostle Paul reflects upon death by inserting the element of sin. When he speaks of exchanging this earthly body for a heavenly one, he exults in the victory over sin. He virtually shouts in this hymn of victory: "O death, where then your victory? Where then your sting? For sin—the sting that causes death—will all be gone; and the law, which reveals our sins, will no longer be our judge" (1 Corinthians 15:54-56, LB). Sin creates the resistance to the exchange of this earthly body for something far superior. The prospect of standing before the judgment of God intimidates us. We see ourselves as criminals because of sin's presence in our lives. We fear condemnation.

The happy truth in Paul's words consists in the fact that as believers the sting of sin is gone. We need not fear the change that must come to inherit the kingdom of God. We go from this world, not to face the condemnation of a Judge, but to be assessed regarding the stewardship of our lives. Jesus brought victory over death. Our judgment as Christ's followers has nothing to do with our destiny, but with our rewards. We go out of this world to a Father who waits for His children to come home. No man qualifies, in his physical state, to inherit the glories of heaven, but neither does any man need to fear the change essential for eligibility to enter God's kingdom.

As I reflect upon my own fears about death, I often resort to one of the passages in the Psalms where David says, "My God in His lovingkindness will meet me" (Psalm 59:10, NAS). The original meaning is that God goes before us. (The King James Version can be confusing with the translation, "The God of my mercy shall prevent me.") The psalmist, therefore, suggests that wherever we go, the Lord always precedes us. In fact, when the same word "prevent" is used in 1 Thessalonians 4:15, it denotes precisely that those who are alive at Christ's coming will not *precede* those who have died. In other words, the psalmist suggests that on every road we travel while walking through the valley of the shadow of death, we find Jesus has already walked there. He will meet us at every corner.

Joni Eareckson, whose dive into Chesapeake Bay paralyzed her for life, has a beautiful passage in her book *A Step Further* about what going to heaven means. As a teenager she abounded with energy and enthusiasm. She loved the outdoors and sports. She was adept at playing hockey. Today she finds herself confined to a wheelchair. In describing her idea of going to heaven she says:

I think of a time when I will be welcomed home. I remember when I was on my feet what a cozy wonderful feeling it was to come home after hockey practice. How pleasant to hear the fa-

miliar clanging of bells against our back door as I swung it
open. Inside awaited the sights, sounds, and smells of warmth
and love. Mom would greet me with a wide smile as she dished
out food into big bowls ready to be set on the table. I'd throw
down my sweat suit and hockey stick, bound into the den, and
greet Daddy. He'd turn from his desk, taking off his glasses,
then he'd give me a big 'hi' and ask me how practice was. For
Christians heaven will be like that.°

Earthly life provides the practice field. When we exchange this body for a heavenly one, the Father and Jesus,
our elder Brother, will greet us. They will ask us how it went
on the practice field. We won't feel insecure and strange.
We will feel at home because that is precisely where we will
be. Like a crippled quadriplegic throwing her arms around
her loving Father, we have the prospect of being gathered
into the arms of a loving Father who loved us even when we
were spiritual quadriplegics.

Fear of death? Yes, our humanity forces something of that
upon us. But our response should be that of the apostle
when he breaks out into joy and celebration with the words:
"How we thank God for all of this! It is he who makes us vic-
torious through Jesus Christ our Lord!" (1 Corinthians
15:57, LB).

No Rest as We Await Change

The biblical view mandates that no man rests as he waits
for the change that ushers him into the kingdom of God.
The temptation to "throw in the towel" after a loved one
passes from our grasp besieges many people. But waiting for
moving day (from tent to temple) means that we remain ac-
tively at work. Death in the family tends to immobilize

°Joni Eareckson and Steve Estes, A *Step Further* (Grand Rapids: Zondervan, 1978).

people for a time, but the biblical view calls for returning to our duties.

The Scripture plainly states: "So, my dear brothers, since future victory is sure, be strong and steady, always abounding in the work of the Lord, for you know that nothing you do for the Lord is ever wasted as it would be if there were no resurrection" (1 Corinthians 15:58, LB). We do not sit around idly when death strikes terror in our hearts. Our task, even in the midst of the pain of parting, requires that we go back to our tasks, being strong and steady, always abounding in our work.

David demonstrates so admirably the proper way to grieve and then return to work. His precious little son lay very ill. He fasted and lay on the ground all night. The child died, and David's servants feared to tell him. David sensed death had taken its toll. He asked for an answer, and he received the sad news. The boy was dead. The next action of David fascinates me. "So David arose from the ground, washed, anointed himself, and changed his clothes; and he came into the house of the Lord and worshiped. Then he came to his own house, and when he requested, they set food before him and he ate" (2 Samuel 12:20, NAS).

His servants stood astonished. First he fasted and wept. Now he washed and ordered food. They asked why. David answered: "While the child was still alive, I fasted and wept; for I said, 'Who knows, the Lord may be gracious to me, that the child may live.' But now he has died; why should I fast? Can I bring him back again? I shall go to him, but he will not return to me" (2 Samuel 12:22-23, NAS).

Pondering the poetic words of the Apostle Paul teaches me that I return to work after grieving. That is not to say that all grief ceases. David no doubt often grieved over the loss of that son. But once the child died, he returned to the normal duties of life. No man rests while he waits for moving day into the eternal kingdom of God.

Our bodies need changing before we can enter that kingdom. We need not fear that change because it is a glorified "coming home." And we work while we wait.

I am home in heaven, dear ones;
　　Oh, so happy and so bright!
There is perfect joy and beauty
　　In this everlasting light.

All the pain and grief are over:
　　Every restless tossing passed;
I am now at peace forever,
　　Safely home in heaven at last!

Did you wonder I so calmly
　　Trod the valley of the shade?
Ah, but Jesus' love illumined
　　Every dark and fearful glade.

And He came Himself to meet me
　　In that way so hard to tread;
And with Jesus' arm to lean on,
　　Could I have no doubt to dread?

Then you must not grieve so sorely,
　　For I love you dearly still:
Try to look beyond earth's shadows
　　Pray to trust our Father's will.

There is work still waiting for you,
　　So you must not idly stand;
Do it now, while life remaineth,
　　You shall rest in Jesus' land.

When that work is all completed
　　He will gently call you home:
Oh the rapture of that meeting!
　　Oh the joy to see you come!
　　　　　　　　　　—Author Unkown

22

Life and Death as Metamorphosis

Almost every fall a fascinating phenomenon occurs in our little south central Kansas town. Monarch butterflies travel through our area on their journey to warmer winter climates. For several days they invade the community by the millions. Their flight appears so leisurely and directionless that one would never guess they are on a five-thousand-mile trip. They dart up and down, back and forth, but if you watch closely, you soon discern that their ultimate movement is always southward. Since we are in the path the monarchs usually follow in their annual trek, we witness a part of their fabulous journey. They sometimes rest for the night in trees to such an extent that the tree is one huge, blazing, orange-colored bush.

Who are these butterflies? From where do they come and what is their destination? Can such a fragile-appearing insect actually fly that far and then return in the spring? The monarch spends the summer anywhere from the Midwest to the north in Canada. The flight pattern that brings them through our town terminates deep into Old Mexico where they winter. They return in the spring but never make the trip again. The parent monarchs die after the return trip and their children repeat the cycle. The whole story is made possible because of what the scientists call metamorphosis.

You or your children likely have watched the mysterious unfolding of life represented by metamorphosis. An ugly, clumsy, wiggling caterpillar becomes a beautiful, graceful butterfly. Metamorphosis transforms one type of life into another. It is one of nature's prime exhibits of change.

The Bible utilizes the principle of metamorphosis in an interesting passage that deserves study when we reflect on death and life. "And we all, with unveiled face, beholding the glory of the Lord, are being changed into his likeness from one degree of glory to another; for this comes from the Lord who is the Spirit" (2 Corinthians 3:18, RSV).

The expression translated "are being changed" in the Greek language is literally a form of the word "metamorphosis." The pilgrimage we call life and the change occurring throughout life is termed as metamorphosis by the Apostle Paul. Spiritual change in God's children is described in the same terms as we speak of changes in the world of nature.

Change Is Part of Our Glory

The ability to change constitutes part of the glory with which we have been created. Upon serious reflection it seems rather strange that the very thing that makes our highest glory possible—change—finds so much resistance in us.

Parents would be intensely dissatisfied if their newborn children remained infants. Mothers often bemoan the fact that their offspring change so rapidly and leave the home so quickly. But one of the saddest misfortunes in a family is the absence of change in a child. We weep figuratively when children mature so quickly, but we weep literally if a child remains a child and never develops into maturity.

Somehow we associate *change* with *decay*. We link the fact that we change with the unwelcome prospect of aging. Maturity all too soon leaves us with the connotation of death. We perceive the connection between change and decay much like the song writer put it:

> Swift to its close ebbs out life's little day;
> Earth's sorrows dim, its glories pass away;
> *Change and decay* in all around I see;
> O Thou who changest not, abide with me.
> —Henry Lyte

Research dispels some of the misunderstandings that prevail among us about aging. As an adult ages his learning ability does not decline appreciably, but remains about the same. Unlike popular perceptions that the majority of people over 65 are confined to institutions, the actual figure is only 5 percent. Nearly 75 percent of older, retired Americans testify to being satisfied with their retirement. Only 25 percent of working Americans express that kind of contentment about their jobs. Most older people do not eventually become financial burdens to their children. The health status of retired persons actually tends to improve after retirement. And fewer than 3 percent of people up to age 70 are considered senile.

A group recently expressed surprise when I presented these facts. This surprise says something about our views on aging and death, for we resent and often resist change. We often look upon change as evil and a sentence. But the Bible

suggests that the possibility of change is a unique characteristic that constitutes part of our glory.

What if our bodies were incapable of change? What if our
minds could not be changed? What if our understanding
remained forever the same? The truth to be faced is that the
absence of change would make it impossible to be altered in
respects that we treasure very much.

Without change it would be impossible to be transformed
from enslavement to sin and freedom in Christ. Without
change it would be impossible for men to move from pleasing themselves to accepting themselves as servants or
stewards of God. Inability to change would negate all possibilities for being born anew. Absence of change would
condemn all of us to sin and confirm us in our guilt. Change
makes possible for God's creatures to be "changed into His
likeness from one degree of glory to another" (2 Corinthians,
3:18, NAS)

Change Is Divinely Initiated

The ability to change spiritually is divinely initiated. Mo-
mentum for spiritual metamorphosis begins with God, not
with ourselves. "We all, with unveiled face, beholding the
glory of the Lord, are *being changed*" (2 Corinthians 3:18,
RSV). Our transformation into genuine, more Christlike
believers does not begin with us. The impetus for change
rests with God. He acts upon us.

As we reflect upon the changes God desires to perform in
our lives, we ought not to assume a complete passiveness.
When the apostle speaks of being changed he does employ a
passive voice verb. But the context insists that we are acted
upon only as we gaze or behold. We change as we behold
the glory of the Lord. Beholding His glory demands a steady
gazing upon the person and character of Christ. Being

transformed into Christ's image—becoming a reflection of Him—imposes upon us the responsibility to focus attention upon Him.

"Boot-strap religion" found no place in Paul's theology. Self-made men and women never entered the apostle's thoughts. The transformation of our lives is spiritually initiated, but not without our cooperation.

But who has time to reflect? We lead such busy, active lives in such a hectic world. Where can one find time to "waste" in a contemplative mood? We choose for our motto "let us then be up and doing," rather than "be still and know that I am God." But being changed *into His likeness* occurs only when our gaze has been fixed upon Him.

In Florence, Italy, in the Academia, there are displayed some ugly, rough blocks of marble called "The Prisoners." They are pieces of marble on which the talented Michelangelo once labored. He never finished any of them. In each block you can see emerging forms, but still imprisoned in the stone. The final product appears to be waiting for the touch of the master's hand to set them free.

As we reflect upon life we see ourselves in a similar fashion—rough hunks of dull, unpolished, unfinished material. But we hold the potential for reflecting the image of Christ. God calls us to allow the Master to touch us, remake us, mold us, to bring out of the rough rocks the full character we are meant to be. God initiates the metamorphosis; we respond.

Change Is Expected in This Life

Spiritual metamorphosis occurs not simply at the close of earthly life, but *during* our earthly pilgrimage. The monarch butterfly's metamorphosis qualifies him not for his exit from this life, but for activity and life. The insect's fuller life, made possible through the miraculous change called meta-morphosis, enhances its life. Change gives freedom to fly rather than crawl.

Too many people who call themselves Christians wait passively for the sudden, drastic change the Bible suggests will occur when they die or the Lord comes in His glory. We conceive of change as something that remains for the future.

On the contrary, the Bible is replete with evidence that spiritual metamorphosis not only is possible but expected in this present life. Sinners changed to saints! Liars trans-formed into truthful persons! Thieves revolutionized into sharers of their goods! Blasphemers turned into people who praise God!

We can't afford to wait until the next world for a spiritual metamorphosis. God's dream for us is change here and now. Too often we defer to the afterlife the things God has planned for us now. With wistful, melancholy eyes we dream of the future day when orderliness and fruitfulness and wholeness shall characterize our beings. We don't have to wait.

The Bible says, "Things which eye has not seen and ear has not heard, and which have not entered the heart of man, all that God has prepared for those who love Him" (1 Corin-thians 2:9, NAS). When? After death? In heaven? No! Here and now!

I have had the good fortune to watch some of the finest people in the world mature, age, and then depart to be with Christ. Fortunately, many of them recognized the possibility of being changed in this life, as well as in the next. I recall with pleasure the life of a widow whose sweet, pleasant spirit was evident to all. No generation gap separated her from her grandchildren and young people in general. Complaints rarely came from her lips. Advancing age added wrinkles but not whimpering and grumbling. Spiritual metamorphosis continued unabated in her life. She was, indeed, *being* changed.

What enables such change to occur? In the case of the sweet old lady I have just described, I'm persuaded it began the day she consciously, deliberately made a decision to follow Christ. To use the Apostle Paul's words, metamorphosis began when the veil was removed. The presence of Christ infiltrated her being and she never ceased changing. At the point of her conversion she became a new creature. But perfection did not happen in one bold stroke. The spiritual metamorphosis continued throughout her earthly life.

The Bible describes this metamorphosis in our salvation. It says we *are* saved, we are *being* saved, and we *shall* be saved. The verb tenses that make this so clear are not always so precisely translated in our English versions, but the Greek language clearly indicates this to be the case. The Bible says there comes a point at which we commit our lives to Christ. Redemption takes place at that moment. But another dimension of our salvation continues, and in this life. We are *being* saved. The process of becoming more and more like Christ continues as we live here and now.

Ultimate Change Occurs at Death

Ultimate spiritual change takes place at the end of our life on earth. I have suggested that the Bible says "we *shall* be saved." Reality demands the admission that the process of spiritual metamorphosis is not finalized in this life. In that respect we differ vastly from the monarch butterfly. Metamorphosis transforms him into a beautiful insect that allows him the freedom of flight for a time. But when death comes, the monarch is finished. He falls to the ground. He returns

to the earth, as do our physical bodies. But nothing
continues for the monarch except decay.

In contrast to the butterfly's future, the Bible describes
our destiny in these words: "Beloved, we are God's children
now; it does not yet appear what we shall be, but we know
that when he appears we shall be like him, for we shall see
him as he is" (1 John 3:2, ASV). Ultimate metamorphosis occurs the moment we meet Christ. Today we reflect something of the image of Christ. Daily we change from one
degree to another toward His likeness. But in Christ's
presence we reach the climax of that glory. The ultimate
glory is to be like Jesus.

Several years ago I was flying over the San Joaquin Valley
in California. Not having anything else to do, I reached for
the airline magazine available in the pocket in front of me.
In that periodical I read the story of a second-grade teacher
in Annapolis, Maryland, who brought a chrysalis, or cocoon,
to her classroom. She had no way of knowing whether or not
it was dead or alive. The next day, however, she and her fascinated pupils knew they were dealing with something alive.
Metamorphosis had taken place. From the dim, gray, wiggly
cocoon emerged a beautiful monarch butterfly. The students were concerned about the little creature's fate. The
not-too-balmy Atlantic Coast weather promised a poor
habitat for the fledgling little butterfly. So the class planned
their strategy. They packed the winged beauty in a box, took
it to the local United Airlines office at Friendship International Airport in Baltimore, and entrusted their prized new
friend to an airlines hostess. She promised to release the butterfly in San Francisco.

The story didn't end there. When the plane arrived in the
bay area, rain descended steadily and the hostess didn't have
the heart to release the fragile little creature in those ele-

ments. So she persuaded a hostess on another flight to take her frail shipment to the beautiful resort city of Monterey. There the happy monarch butterfly soared into a sunnier and friendlier sky.

Reflecting upon death and life as God sees it, the stage we call "life" represents the cocoon stage. Not that earthly life is "grubby" and dull, but in comparison to what our ultimate change will be, life here and now dimly foreshadows the glory we will possess in the presence of Christ. This life holds its beauties, but the days are sometimes clouded by not-so-balmy weather. But one day, when the release of death comes, like the freed monarch butterfly, our spirits will be released into a sunnier, friendlier, and more beautiful life. Spiritual metamorphosis culminates in the presence of Christ.

Marvin Hein was pastor of Hillsboro Mennonite Brethren Church in Kansas for more than twenty years. His meditations on death and life are drawn from his experience with this congregation, as well as from his wide reading, academic studies, and church leadership. In 1980 he moved to California to pastor the North Fresno Mennonite Brethren Church.

A graduate of Tabor College in Hillsboro (AB in Bible and history) and Central Baptist Theological Seminary (ThM) in Kansas City, Kansas, Hein also spent 1975 in sabbatical studies at Fuller Theological Seminary. From 1956-1978 he taught at Tabor College.

Marvin Hein is a North American vice-president of the Mennonite World Conference. He has served as chairman of the General Conference of Mennonite Brethren Churches (1969-1975); chairman of the Board of Christian Education of the United States Conference of Mennonite Brethren Churches; and chairman of the Board of Herald Publishing Company (*Mennonite Weekly Review*).

He has written for Brethren, Mennonite, and Friends periodicals and is the author of *The Ties That Bind* (Kindred Press, 1980). Hein and his wife, Mary Helen, are the parents of three children: Patricia, Penelope, and Holly.